To My Ex[...]
Jim —

A conversational
portrait of a modern
(postmodern?) moderate
Muslim Machiavelli —
who kept up the
balancing act for
22 years — no
explosions!
Cheers,
Tom Plate

GIANTS *of* ASIA

DOCTOR M:
OPERATION
MALAYSIA

conversations with

MAHATHIR
MOHAMAD

TOM PLATE

Marshall Cavendish
Editions

Cover illustration by P.K. Cheng. Design by Bernard Go Kwang Meng.
Research by My Lu. Photographs by Tom Plate.

Published by Marshall Cavendish Editions
An imprint of Marshall Cavendish International
1 New Industrial Road, Singapore 536196

Other Marshall Cavendish Offices
Marshall Cavendish Ltd. PO Box 65829, London EC1P INY, UK • Marshall Cavendish
Corporation. 99 White Plains Road, Tarrytown NY 10591-9001, USA • Marshall Cavendish
International (Thailand) Co Ltd. 253 Asoke, 12th Flr, Sukhumvit 21 Road, Klongtoey Nua,
Wattana, Bangkok 10110, Thailand • Marshall Cavendish (Malaysia) Sdn Bhd, Times Subang,
Lot 46, Subang Hi-Tech Industrial Park, Batu Tiga, 40000 Shah Alam, Selangor Darul Ehsan,
Malaysia.

Marshall Cavendish is a trademark of Times Publishing Limited

National Library Board Singapore Cataloguing in Publication Data

Plate, Tom.
Conversations with Mahathir Mohamad : Doctor M : operation Malaysia / Tom Plate. –
Singapore : Marshall Cavendish Editions, c2011.
p. cm. – (Giants of Asia)
Includes bibliographical references.
ISBN : 978-981-4276-63-4

1. Mahathir bin Mohamad, 1925- – Interviews. 2. Mahathir bin Mohamad, 1925- – Political
and social views. 3. Mahathir bin Mohamad, 1925- – Religion. 4. Prime ministers – Malaysia –
Interviews. I. Title. II. Series: Giants of Asia.

DS597.215
959.5054092 -- dc22   OCN693757660

Printed in Singapore by KWF Printing Pte Ltd

Asked what they thought about **DR MAHATHIR MOHAMAD** and his legacy, here are what these world figures and experts had to say.

"When the economy was growing rapidly, most Malaysians were willing to ignore the darker side of Mahathir's one-man rule: the no-bid contracts awarded to cronies, the lack of transparency, the restrictions on political freedom, the decline in Malaysia's educational system and quality of governance, and the squandering of public monies on failed projects from Proton to Perwaja to Putrajaya. But no more. Still, 'Dr M' is a fascinating figure— controversial, outspoken, and never boring. He ranks with Tunku Abdul Rahman as Malaysia's most transformational leader. Long before Barack Obama, he was telling his people 'yes, we can.' (*Malaysia boleh.*) His legacy will be that of a bold, visionary, but ultimately flawed leader."

John R. Malott,
U.S. Ambassador to Malaysia, 1995–98

"Dr Mahathir Mohamad is an international figure who still exerts a great influence in many fields. His achievements are recognized not only at the Malaysian level. He has demonstrated how persistence, hard work and vision are omnipotent to guarantee success. His rare sense of patriotism and moderate religious beliefs have played a major role in his openness to other cultures and to his keen interest to develop the education process in Malaysia and to make it more accessible to the population. His political and development approach is considered by many politicians and leaders as a model reflecting his deep commitment to create a just and equal society.

Dr Mahathir Mohamad is a strong proponent of moderate Islam and has practically proved how Islam, when understood well and implemented correctly, can be a driving factor for development and progress. He is a man who believes that Islam can be integrated into all affairs of life and is compatible with the universal concepts of justice and human rights. This is reflected in his ability to evolve coexistence between different religions and ethnic groups in Malaysia and in his respect for others' beliefs."

His Excellency Dr Abu Baker Al-Qirbi,
Minister of Foreign Affairs, the Republic of Yemen

"He was an outstanding Prime Minister of Malaysia. During his premiership of over 20 years, he changed Malaysia from an agricultural, placid society into an industrial, dynamic society. He educated his people, sent many abroad on scholarships. They in turn transformed Malaysia."

Lee Kuan Yew,
Prime Minister of Singapore, 1959–90

"When Tun Dr Mahathir became Prime Minister of Malaysia in the early 1980s, I was a Deputy Secretary in the Ministry of Finance. The country and civil service in particular were initially impressed by his quiet charisma and his strong leadership and decisive qualities. He inspired us with many of his innovative policies like the Look East Policy, Malaysia Incorporated, Buy British Last, and so on. Many of us were also moved by his nationalistic stance in international fora over economic, trade, investment, financial, diplomatic, security, and environmental policies. On the domestic front, great strides were taken to stimulate economic growth and strengthen the national infrastructure in the country. We were struck by the new modern highways, the new airport, the world-class Twin Towers, and the new national capital called Putrajaya. Many believed that Dr Mahathir really put Malaysia on the global map, and we were proud of it!

However, as he continued his long rule of 22 years, we slowly began to feel uneasy with the price we were paying for his authoritarian style of government. His overly critical and aggressive approach to the Western world, which provided us with export markets and foreign direct investment, lost us some international goodwill. In championing the legitimate concerns of South and Middle East countries, forcefully and sometimes even abrasively, he created considerable negative reactions against Malaysia that did not help. Internally the strong national institutions that we had inherited from the British at the time of Independence in 1957 began to weaken under Dr Mahathir's watch. The judiciary in particular, the civil service, the police and the education system, inter alia, gradually declined. Indeed the whole administrative system began to sag under the burden of growing corruption and money politics. Furthermore, his undue commitment to restructuring equity ownership for the *bumiputras* caused some loss in efficiency, integrity and meritocracy, and competitiveness in the whole socio-economic system of the country. To a large extent the abuses that occurred during his stewardship, due to the improper implementation of many aspects of the New Economic Policy, increased racial and religious polarization and made Malaysia lose some of its shine and image as a successful multireligious and multiracial country. Tun Dr Mahathir's legacy would be much more creditable if his many achievements in the international arena and in developing our domestic infrastructure could have been enhanced by his building up strong institutions, rather than weakening them. If he had done so, Malaysia would be a much better, more united, and more progressive country, and a real example of a successful multiracial-religious country."

Tan Sri Ramon Navaratnam,
former Deputy Secretary, Ministry of Finance, Malaysia

"Citizen Mahathir is an enigma and iconoclast. In my view, he has in retirement become a deeply mischievous and superbly entertaining egoist. It is the brute power of his ego that had driven him onwards and upwards. The word 'ego' holds no shame or fear for him. From a modest and compassionate medicine man (some of his close friends call him Bomoh) with a thriving medical practice in Kedah, he rose to become the most powerful Prime Minister of Malaysia for 22 years, breaking all social and other barriers. He evokes affection and admiration and also condemnation and scorn from Malaysians. Even in the autumn of his years, he continues to badger and pique the new generations of leaders, an act he would not have tolerated when he held power. I admired him as an intellectual, a professional manager, and businessman. But his politics were perplexing to me. He was to me and men and women of my generation, the first among equals, who held the promise of a new dawn for Malaysia. When he became Prime Minister in 1981, most of us were excited with his leadership by example and the idea of a clean, efficient and trustworthy government. It was amazing that Mahathir had become in one brief moment in time a liberal democrat. Things began to change mid-stream when he launched a massive crackdown on his political enemies and dissidents in 1987 and created a new UMNO [leading political party] which he could control absolutely. As political supremo, he went on to emasculate all institutions of governance, especially the judiciary and the civil service. He amended the constitution, created an all-powerful Executive Branch, and destroyed the system of checks and balances. A nascent Malaysian democracy was replaced by an authoritarian leader who ran the country his way.

Even his bitter critics would, however, not deny that Mahathir was a man of action who was unafraid to do what he thought was in the interest of his country. He was a risk-taker and a man who would not allow opposition to stall his agenda as embodied in his Vision 2020. He transformed the economy from an agricultural backwater into a modern manufacturing and industrial metropolis, but he also deformed the Malaysian polity. That is a tragedy, and

Malaysia is today in a moral crisis of sorts. Citizen Mahathir is not the man I once knew and admired. Power, absolute power changed him. In fact, I see him as a tragic figure who is unable to let go. What is worse is that he has regressed to become the Malay ultra that he once was in the 1960s. Let us hope history will be kinder to him when future generations of scholars and researchers examine his record as our longest serving Prime Minister."

Din Merican, former Malaysian diplomat,
businessman, central banker and academic

"For a long time, Dr Mahathir seemed the only Muslim leader in the world with an information age vision of the future instead of an obsession with the past. Moreover, he had done much for his country, raising his people from poverty and widening the middle class, while preventing inter-ethnic conflict like the anti-Chinese pogroms that have bloodied other Asian streets over the years. Regrettably, Dr Mahathir's vision seemed to lose credibility with the Anwar Ibrahim affair. Instead of a sound strategy to compete in the global information age, Dr Mahathir seemed to have adopted the tactics of a police state with the arrest and ill-treatment of Anwar, his second in command while prime minister. Unfortunately, that terrible episode threatens to destroy the historic legacy of the many positive achievements Dr Mahathir brought to his country."

Alvin and Heidi Toffler,
authors of Future Shock, The Third Wave *and many others*

Thanking those who helped make this book possible

Former Malaysian Prime Minister Mahathir Mohamad, the subject of this second volume in the "Giants of Asia" series, was continually pleasant and cooperative in our four sessions of conversations, and seemed to want to help me make this book as real and helpful as possible. He will not of course remotely agree with all the judgments in this volume but I hope he accepts that everything in this work aims to be fair and honest.

Chris Newson, the imaginative and energetically hands-on general manager of Marshall Cavendish Asia, is one determined man—and a great pleasure to work with. His super editors **Violet Phoon** and **Lee Mei Lin** are so sharp—as good as any in the book business anywhere, in my experience. They bring balance, integrity, caring and solid judgment to difficult and important material. I would be lost without them and I am looking forward to working with them on the next GIANT.

My (Mimi) Lu, now a recently-credentialed U.S. Foreign Service Officer and recent graduate of the Fletcher School of Law and Diplomacy, via UCLA, where she was the teachingassistant in my classes, was the chief researcher on this book, as she was on its predecessor; and she has been my right-hand almost-everything these past half dozen years. Thanks, as well, to **Theron Raines**, of Raines & Raines, who has been a most patient literary agent.

Reading an earlier draft were true friends and colleagues: **Nathan Gardels**, the preeminent U.S. international journalist, media entrepreneur (Global Viewpoints, New Perspectives Quarterly) and intellectually elegant internationalist; and **Mark Kleiman**, the outstanding drug-policy analyst (author of the thoroughly brilliant *When Brute Force Fails*, Princeton University Press, 2009) and a truly exceptional UCLA public-affairs professor. Both made superb suggestions and I did my best to integrate them but of course the views and conclusions are entirely my own responsibility.

Last and anything but least, **Andrea Darvi Plate**, who helped me sort out the difficult issue of Mahathir and the Jews, while suffering through my long periods of self-absorption: somehow, against all odds, she is still my glorious wife.

To

*The professors of my youth, at Amherst College and
Princeton University's Woodrow Wilson School, without whose
challenge and encouragement to think deeply and write carefully no
book of even the slightest possible value would ever have been written.*

*Especially and including:
the late Benjamin DeMott
Richard Falk
the late Roy Health
George Kateb
the late Earl Latham
the late C. Scott Porter
William Harrison Pritchard
the late Theodore Sorensen
Richard Ullman*

Thank you all: I would be nowhere without you.

Contents

Dr Mahathir and the author at the former prime minister's office in Petronas Tower 1 (September 2009)

Prelude:
How 'Dr No' Became 'Dr Yes'

**The beginning of four conversations,
in Kuala Lumpur or Putrajaya, with the former
Prime Minister of Malaysia (1981–2003)**

LOVE him or hate him, support him or fight him, worship him or damn him, he was a giant of Asia.

For 22 years, he helped raise Malaysia out of an equatorial lassitude of nothingness and push it up onto the world stage as a player everyone in the global-know recognized.

At home, he helped make sure his beloved country didn't miss the forward thrust of the rollicking freight train known as the Asian Economic Miracle. Between 1981 and 2003—his years as prime minister—the Gross National Product of this otherwise obscure Southeast Asian and largely Muslim nation more than quadrupled. In some years the annual growth rate flirted with 10 percent, almost unheard of for the land of the mellow Malays.

But Dr Mahathir Mohamad was no one-dimensional man. At times he would move as silently as a river around rocks, slipping far downstream before anyone realized just how far he had gone. At other times he was an egg smasher who'd crack open clusters of political opposition and fry them into pitiless, helpless omelets—a monster-sized personality, at times a stalker at center stage whom no one could ignore.

Just as Lee Kuan Yew for more than three decades was the omnipresent public face of Singapore, Dr Mahathir was the maestro of modernizing Malaysia for more than two.

Lee was the pragmatic conceptualist, drawing on his classical Cambridge education while behaving almost as if a stern, logical positivist who'd miraculously gotten a little country to prove or disprove his economic-development and governance ideas.

Mahathir was more of the folksy country doctor (which once in fact he had been), toting around his doctor's bag stuffed with quick fixes, experimental elixirs and just about anything that might quell political fever, restore the body politic to vigorous economic health and/or entice the patient to ask him to remain his or her doc for life.

It helped the framing of the dominant political personality of the first book in this "Giants of Asia" series, *Conversations With Lee Kuan Yew*, to draw on the legendary analogy of the late Sir Isaiah Berlin. His 1953 essay "The Hedgehog and the Fox" divided great men/women into two categories, based on the insight of the ancient Greek poet Archilochus: "The fox knows many little things, but the hedgehog knows one big thing."

In my book on the founder of modern Singapore, I put Lee Kuan Yew into the hedgehog category, even though he stoutly resisted most of the way, claiming he was a pragmatic fox who abhorred grand conceptualizations (out of a very understandable generic fear of political ideologies).

But categorizing Dr Mahathir requires no comparable intellectual struggle: the man is an Isaiah Berlin fox, a political survivor and national leader of a million little different moves and tricks … for 22 years, in effect, the conjuring magician of Malaysia.

So let's meet him.

Walking in, I re-introduce myself.

From behind the desk, in an olive-green safari-style jacket, the former political master of Malaysia (himself well-known for baiting Western journalists) could scarcely restrain himself. He looked at me almost as if he didn't recognize me.

And maybe he didn't, for it was ten years ago that we had met in New York at a World Economic Forum confab, and before that in Davos.

So I say: "You know me—the career American journalist."

Not two blinks go by and he quips: "That's too bad … but no one is perfect!"

Vintage Mahathir.

A part of me secretly agreed with his dour view of my semi-disreputable profession, and I think he knew it, which is partly why he said it.

Then, in an almost pretentious preamble, I say, rather carefully and speaking slowly (though his English is first-rate, his hearing good and his mind, as you will see, still sharp in its mid-eighties):

"This book—it's not a traditional political biography with a million words and a thousand footnotes and a dozen hidden axes to grind. It's the reader having a long and maybe somewhat intimate conversation with Dr M. The idea is to feel his personality, his flair, his instincts, his brain. Nobody else is like you. Lee Kuan Yew of Singapore is different from you. You are different from Japan's Nakasone or from Thailand's Thaksin or from America's Clinton or from Germany's Merkel or Russia's Putin."

What I don't say to him—no sense trying to butter him up—is that as the only famous *Muslim* leader in that bunch, Mahathir in these tense and perilous times is, arguably, as important an historical figure as any of the above.

I continue, in cautious manner: "The heart of this book is what you say to me, most importantly—and what I say to you, much less importantly. The only thing I recommend is, be yourself and I'll just ask my questions. I can ask you anything, right?"

He nods almost absent-mindedly, giving off the aura of being able to run this country of 26 million mostly Muslims even today.

For this session, he is sitting behind a big oak desk on the second floor of something akin to what in the U.S. we might regard as a cluster of presidential libraries. It's called the Perdana Leadership Foundation, which came into being near the end of Mahathir's long run, and which aims to be a combination honorarium for past prime ministers and a scholarly sanitarium for their records and papers.

I plow on: "If you say anything that you later want to pull

back—but I don't think you are like this—you should know I'm very probably going to be okay with that and will honor that. Everyone should be relaxed. This isn't a 'gotcha' kind of interview. I'm not interested in your secret Nazi past."

Dr M suddenly stirs and brightens. It's as if this light, goofy (almost offensive) touch of mine serves to lift his spirit somehow, as if, whatever the allegations of corruption and authoritarian harshness hovering over his legacy, anyone who would invoke the faintest reference to Nazis would obviously have to be joking.

Giving back as he usually does, he cracks: "So you know all about it!"

Thunderball!

Meeting the West's journalists … the Davos sessions … Muslim terrorism … beating Wall Street

READERS should know where the writer is coming from and so we need to begin with a story. It tries to explain why Dr Mahathir deserves to be taken seriously, despite his penchant for putting things out there that almost no one takes seriously.

This is the last diversion before we head straight to the contemporary conversations with Mahathir.

Personally, I try to ignore what is said for effect so as to benefit from what we can learn when he is striving for truth, not effect. And he has been right on so many major issues, it's almost hard to think of many other leaders of his generation who come close to him in correct-prognostication percentage. More than almost any other national leader one can think of, for example, he was right about the destabilizing danger of capital flows and the need to reform our international financial architecture.

Let's go back to 2002, to a famous conference in a famous world city that took place after the infamous bludgeoning of America known everywhere as 9/11. The scene was the World Economic Forum's annual conference, attended by close to 2,000 of the (mainly) Western world's movers and shakers. This took place in Manhattan. The host venue was the historic and grandiose, if aging, Waldorf-Astoria Hotel.

One of the visiting VIP movers-shakers was then Prime Minister Mahathir Mohamad. Malaysia had just recently emerged onto the international stage—and into people's consciousness—as a rapidly developing economy. Today it ranks on the economic totem pole with countries such as Chile, Mexico and Turkey. Not so many years before Mahathir, it was a dusty Third World forget-about-it that ranked basically nowhere.

But what was then under-appreciated is that governing a mostly Muslim country is not the same as governing a secular nation. What was then and still is not fully appreciated is that in this age of Islamic terrorism, the former family doctor had for two decades somehow managed a Muslim nation almost notorious for not being remotely notorious.

For he will not admit to it, and indeed if you try to call him a 'moderate Muslim' he will almost vehemently deny it, but for all his faults as a leader, whatever we and/or others find them to be, and whatever Malaysia's faults as a nation, and like all nations it has many, he was in fact the best living example of an effective moderate-Muslim leader that in recent memory the world had seen.

But, of course, he gets little recognition for that.

We were just beginning to understand that after 9/11.

The sprawling Waldorf-Astoria was a complete zoo. VIPs from all over the world were scurrying around like bees at a new hive.

They were being pursued by journalists from all over, but especially from the self-important Washington-New York media corridor.

No one was pursuing Mahathir. Hardly anyone in the Washington-New York media axis then knew much about him, except for his well-reported verbal attacks in the late 90s on George Soros and other 'Jewish financiers' for their profit-driven assaults on Asian currencies and stocks, including Malaysia's, during the infamous Asian Financial Crisis.

In 1999, Mahathir had spoken out at the annual World Economic Forum conference held in the freezing Swiss alps of Davos (except in 2002, out of respect for Manhattan's 9/11 suffering). There he had defended his unorthodox cosseting of the Malaysian ringgit, the national currency, with confident aplomb.

This was when his daring and imagination were under scathing attack by Western media defenders of Wall Street, such as the *Wall Street Journal, Fortune Magazine* and many others. But in my *Los Angeles Times* column I tended to agree with his views. That was because, on this issue at least, he was right: "No one anywhere has concluded that our currency measures have been a spectacular failure," as he slyly put it back then.

So when it was arranged at the conference that the Malaysian delegation would offer a private briefing to a group of Western journalists, eight of us quickly signed up, especially when word got out that Mahathir was to lead the delegation.

Malaysia's controversial prime minister—one foot out the PM door but still in power—was no shrinking violet, of course. Still, it was a surprise that he would expose himself to what would surely be a hostile audience. Especially on the East Coast, if the media thought anything about Dr M at all, it was that the head of Malaysia was a dangerous loose cannon ... and probably an anti-Semite. For the East Coast news media of the United States of America, such a reputation will guarantee blanket hostility, to put it mildly.

Waiting with my fellow American journalists in a business-conference room at the Waldorf-Astoria Hotel for the Malaysians and their pugilistic PM to show up, I was asked what to expect. There wasn't enough time to brief journalists who knew almost nothing about him. So I made a weak joke, saying something like: "All I can tell you is that they're Malaysians, so they will be late!"

Amid the laughter, I then asked a reporter from a major East Coast newspaper what he thought of Dr Mahathir. His response was so swift and so sure—and so typical: "He's a jerk and an anti-Semite and I assume he's stupid, too, more or less your average Third World Leader."

Whatever Mahathir is, average is not one ... he is not stupid ... and prospering Malaysia was not even back then a Third World country ... so much for facts.

I said nothing, nothing at all, just took a deep breath, and then: "Tell you what. Just listen to him carefully and if at any time during his briefing you have reason to revise that assessment in any way or to any degree, give me a good, hard, meaningful stare, ok?"

The American reporter nodded. He was smug—no climb-down from him. But maybe he wouldn't have to—who knows what

Dr M would do or say? He's unpredictable—always was, probably always will be … right to the grave.

Then suddenly, with personal panache and a splash of aides, Dr M entered. Garbed in a colorful batik shirt, he stood no more than six feet tall but seemed anything but physically frail. He had an air about him of extreme self-confidence. It is only when I get to know him better ten years later that I realize this is armor for some inner insecurity… amid all the extreme self-confidence.

I caught the eye of this modern-day Malaysian Machiavellian. I mumbled a 'hi', then settled down and watched as this doctor of medicine and 'magician' of Malaysia went to work on the journalists. It was something to see. Without hesitation, the PM tore into all the tough issues: 9/11, Afghanistan, Iraq, Islamic terrorism, the then-labeled Bush administration's 'War on Terrorism', the shaky international financial architecture. His command of the facts was encompassing, and his viewpoints electrifying. It was a first-rate briefing.

A sprinkling of astonishment hit the faces of the assembled journalists. Their image of him was that of a dumb Muslim mynah bird with a bad attitude toward the West and a moronic propensity for unnecessary bluntness.

It took a lot for me not to smirk or laugh. This was not the Mahathir they had been told about or had read about or rumored about. Why? It's simple: the Malaysian leader about which they had read was the one about which they had written!

But the correlation between what they thought they knew

(without, in almost all cases, ever meeting the man or actually setting foot in the country) and what was solid in verifiable objective reality was … err … not exactly perfect.

In effect this man who had run Malaysia for two decades plus was in their limited reality nothing more than a total figment of their imaginations—imaginations that were limited by partial information and cultural stereotypes.

So who—really—was this man Mahathir?

Then it came—my glory moment!

Halfway through the 80-minute session, the American reporter shot me a look and I knew what it meant: this Malaysian guy was certainly no posturing Potemkin potentate. *He knew his stuff!*

Later I wandered around the massive hotel ballroom chock-a-block with global VIPs. Among the delegates milling about was Dr M. And he was not only alone but he seemed obviously lonely. So I figured he could do worse than have a few words with me.

I walked over, intending to tell him that his earlier performance with the Western journalists went quite well. I wanted him to know that his breakdown of the Asian Financial Crisis had been full of sharp observations. And also that his prescriptions for handling the Muslim terrorist challenge were insightful and counter-intuitive, among them:

- Don't bomb or invade. Instead be patient, gather up world opinion—it's on your side now, don't waste all that good will;

- Move slowly to identify and isolate the problem areas, while not creating any new enemies or raising doubts about your true intentions, i.e., a new Christian Crusade;

- Okay with going into Afghanistan (he grumbled) but whatever you do, don't go into Iraq and thus play into the hands of your enemies by seeking to occupy not one but two Muslim countries;

- And whatever you do, don't label your problem a 'war on terror'. Because maybe a billion-plus Muslims might wind up taking it personally—and you don't want that. What you are getting into needs to be narrowly defined. You are taking out one militant arm of the Islamic world, and if you do it right (limited damage to civilians; don't make, act or talk as if it is a Christian Crusade … yet another one) you will have well more than half of all Muslims on your side!

The briefing occurred two years after the winding down of the Asian Financial Crisis (1997–99). This was the economic meltdown that drove up unemployment and political instability across the region. Worse yet, Asian economies that played by Wall Street rules were worst hit. Those that insisted on remaining semi-isolated fared the best. Mahathir became famous in Asia (and infamous in America) for defying the Wall Street rules and throwing sand in the face of the so-called Washington Consensus on liberal and open economies. He regarded that consensus and its ideology as a rapacious formula for the degradation of growing, otherwise healthy, but smaller economies … like his own.

And to make him even more irritating to Wall Street, his protective moves worked; and his predictions turned out to be correct.

Dr M's appearance reminded me that we have to understand that the culture of Western banking is not everyone's culture. It is certainly not the brother or the sister of the Islamic banking ethos. That culture claims to prioritize banking that is community-driven, or anchored in social norms: banks should not make profits through the charging of interest, for example, and should not offer money to businesses that market bad or un-Islamic products. Okay, it's not the American way of banking—but must there be only one way?

I finally found him amid the VIP swells, but standing off to the side, alone.

The first thing you generally notice when you approach him are his eyes: they are like a pair of egg yolks. Genetics awarded Mahathir very large eyes and as you move closer to his face, they stand out as almost little innocent globes on a vast well-lined facial tableau of over-confidence, self-doubt, worry and wisdom—all sometimes flavored with just a touch of menace or (alternatively) a childlike innocence, depending on the mood.

"You were very good earlier today," I said. And I meant it.

He looked at me like I'm a Martian.

"Tom Plate, the American journalist," I said, in reminder. "I was at the briefing you gave today. You knocked their socks off."

Still no reaction. I guess 'knocked-off socks' is not a well-known Malaysian folk expression, especially for a folk who often wear sandals.

Again: "Your briefing was terrific … really."

Suddenly he got it, realized I actually meant it, recognized that I had been at the session, and smiled, a huge brilliant moon-over-Manhattan smile. For a moment I thought it one of the warmest smiles I had ever seen.

It was as if East met West, getting along swimmingly. And this chance but iconic meeting, as it happened, turned out to be the beginning of Volume Two in the "Giants of Asia" series.

A Mahathir Political Point

If only Americans would listen more to the people who live in the region they are about to invade, they might think twice about it, and win more friends than if they had blundered on ahead.

Die Another Way?

No-stress Mahathir … a different theory about 9/11?
… coming up short of the conspiracy cliff

IT is near the very end of the first conversation. I have to start at the end so you can see the problem. It may seem odd to launch this book of generally serious conversations by emphasizing the most bizarre exchange of them all. But you'll see the point.

It ended around noon on a typically hot, though not oppressively humid, June day in downtown Kuala Lumpur. I was happy the interview was almost over but I was also sad, because time spent with Dr Mahathir Mohamad in talk and exchange is anything but an exercise in tedium. The political journalist in me doesn't want it to end.

Dr M is a refreshing verbal vacation from the buttoned-up, guarded, candor-less world of the politician who has little to say and even then can scarcely bring himself to say it. He is living history with vivacity.

Mahathir is to the political interview what maybe Shostakovich is to the symphony or a hurricane is to a change in calm weather. Or perhaps, to use a sports analogy: he is more like a roller derby than a golf game. Australian football, not badminton.

His energy is epic. The former family physician turned prime minister was 83 when these conversations began in the summer of 2009, and he was 84 when the fourth and last one was held in May 2010. At the finish, our sessions seemed not to have aged him—the one who aged may have been me! As he later was to put it to me: "I don't feel stress."

I truly believe he doesn't, or not so much. He is self-confident enough, as well as insecure, in the quietly neurotic way of all politicians seeking total love from all in their visage. Sure, our objective was serious and even arguably important: to place in some large context the significance of a man who so dominated Malaysian politics for decades, to get a feel for his often masterful maneuverings within his own multicultural society, and to understand his sense of his relationship to the larger Muslim community in his own country and even beyond its borders.

Despite these considerable stakes, political exposition doesn't have to be a funeral procession. If we censor out his wild (if sometimes entertaining) assertions, would you then take him more seriously? Or would you not be deprived of a missing dimension to this complicated political personality?

My approach is to put almost all of it out there. Fear not the bizarre or unusual. Mahathir himself likes to have some fun by testing all waters, deep or shallow. He is a political fisherman casting his line to hook certifiable jerks into the boat for a good skinning. The only way not to get caught on his line is to go with the flow and sense the tidal waves—or dark undertow—of his many moods. And to be careful of which pieces of his bait you bite at!

You have to be alert because he doesn't mind getting wet himself in pursuit of his prey. He can laugh at himself as well, as long as you let him be the first to laugh.

And be certain to let him be the first to laugh, because then he doesn't feel that you view him as some sort of Malay or Muslim joke. Which would be the end of the conversation.

He certainly doesn't fear trolling in tricky waters. Our multiple conversations touched on many topics around which lesser figures would instinctively navigate a wide berth, for fear of going aground. Let me say this: if you like your politicians blunt and outspoken, Mahathir is hard to dislike. But if you prefer them sweet-talking, punch-pulling and diplomatic, Dr M is not going to be your cup of tea.

And of all his views in this book, surely those about Israel and its Jewish admirers and allies across the globe will be examined most closely.

And that they deserve to be.

During these conversations I was to press him again and again on these points—to give him an opportunity to either clarify his views, or even modify them, because some of them are hard to take, especially for a Westerner like me, married to a Jewish woman, with a splendid (only) child who's by Jewish law therefore technically Jewish, and with far more Jewish friends than, say, Catholic ones. (And in America, you see, anyone who lived in New York City for as long as I did—almost three decades—is virtually viewed as an 'honorary Jew'.)

I put to him this sensitive issue of Mahathir and his views on the Jews in this way: "The other thing, now don't blow your top, don't get mad, but (just to illustrate) there's this liberal professor at a major U.S. university who reflects the views of some other Jews, maybe even many of them. He says, 'So, I'm sure if Dr M were in total control, he'd be getting the gas ovens ready.' And this is a brilliant guy. I said to him, 'Have you ever met Dr Mahathir?' 'No.' 'Ever been to Malaysia?' 'No.' "

Me going on: "How do I deal with this? Because, when I write this book, and I know he'll read it (because he's basically a very good guy and a loyal friend and a brilliant scholar), and others will be reading it, I want American Jews to have a better sense of who you are. Now, maybe you don't care; okay, you don't have to care. You don't have to prove anything. But I care, because I have to put my name on the book! So I really care."

He seems unmoved. For he is, as you will see, stubborn on the issue of saying whatever he wants about Jews while knowing full well he'll trigger a storm. Only once did he begin to beg off and appear to realize he was heading off a cliff.

And this happens at the end of the very first session. It's vital that you know it now, not later. This is when his penchant for driving toward the cliff—James Dean in *Rebel Without a Cause?*—became apparent. (In fact, as a much younger man, he was proud to show off and tool around his rural hometown in an American Buick!)

It comes out when I asked him about another professor: "So there was this professor in the United States named Ward Churchill, who lost his tenured position at the University of Colorado for saying that many of the people killed in 9/11, in those twin World Trade Center buildings, were terrorists ... economic terrorists, Wall Street terrorists. What do you think of that?"

He shifts a little in his seat. When he is pondering, his head will tilt a little to the left as his lips crinkle in a slight smirk to the right.

And then he chooses to answer in what I thought was a strange way: "Well, I wouldn't condemn all of them. There were three Malaysians there who died and they were not terrorists of any sort. I know for a fact. But one of the things that was pointed out is that on that day, there were hardly any Jews in the building. See, this is a question that many people ask: why? Normally, they work on those days."

"Mhm." This seemed a borderline scary assertion, factually inaccurate (in fact, there were hundreds of Jews among the fatalities); but I let it go and asked instead: "Do you read anything into that?"

"I don't know. I have to say that there is something peculiar about it."

"But why would terrorists, Muslim terrorists, want to attack a building that had only a small number of Jews?"

"Well, they should be there, really, because they're working there. On that day, they happened to not be working there."

What he is suggesting, of course, is that what you saw was not what happened. The real bad guys were not the folks you had thought were the bad guys. The complicated idea under conveyance here is: conspiracy within conspiracy.[1]

(And a few months after we finished our series of conversations, he came out with a lulu: that 9/11 itself might not actually have taken place but conceivably could have been a staged event, given the kind of advanced and duplicitous Western technology that was capable of converting a mere movie like Avatar into a semblance of breathtaking 'reality'.)

I catch my own breath and try to stay calm: "I'll have to check on that. I may get back to you on it. Do you want to talk some more about that?"

I really hope he doesn't. If Mahathir is obliquely referring to the ludicrous hypothesis that the government of Israel had secretly orchestrated the 9/11 attacks (i.e., very few Jews were in the WTC buildings because of prior warning about the danger), I will need a very stiff drink—and it was not even noon now.

"No."

---

1 In summary: in 2002, Saudi Interior Minister Prince Nayef said: "We put big question marks and ask who committed the events of September 11 and who benefited from them. I think they (the Zionists) are behind these events." The minister asserted that the suicide bombers did not act alone and al-Qaeda had the help of the Israeli intelligence, especially Mossad. The aim was to turn the world against Islam, Muslims and Arabs. These comments came after conspiracy theorists claimed that very few Jews or Israelis died on 9/11. The reality is that hundreds of Jews and Israelis died in the towers and on the planes and some were among the first Fire and Police Department responders who died when the towers collapsed.

I sighed with enormous relief. I felt we were heading off the cliff for a huge crash. This was not helpful to my sanity.

Do note that it is unusual (we shall learn) for Mahathir to resist discussion about anything. Yet I welcomed the unexpected halt in this particular recklessness. It became one of those rare times in our conversations that I was truly glad to see him pull up, for to doubt his maturity (not to mention his mental health) would not be healthy for the book. Or for my thesis that Mahathir's life and views are of profound relevance today.

What's more, Mahathir and the mainstream Islam he stands for, is far too important to be made a joke of, including (and especially) by himself.

"Okay," I said, sounding, I am sure, greatly relieved: "But could we get … could I get a glass of water?"

Truly, I needed a drink—and something stronger than H2O. But in the presence of a declared Muslim, and at little past 11 in the morning, water would have to do until much later, back at the hotel, in the privacy of my own Western secular liquidated apostasy.

A Mahathir Political Point

**Speech was given to me not so much
as to disguise my thoughts but to
permit me to say exactly what I think.**

A View to Thrill

**Making fast friends ... Petronas Towers syndrome
... why he is Dr Yes ... Cabinet rules**

How to figure out Dr Mahathir Mohamad—complex, wily, contradictory, mean, warm-hearted, brilliant, stumbling, grumbling, open-minded, witty, probably historical, sometimes hysterical?

How to get our arms around this larger-than-life political giant who sometimes ruled Malaysia almost like a spoiled (though incredibly hard-working) brat for 22 years?

Consider: he was the country's longest-running prime minister ever—the equivalent of almost three U.S. presidents going their full two four-year terms!

More than four Korean presidents going their full permissible five-year term!

Three consecutive French presidents, each going their constitutional seven-year term!

Almost three different United Nations secretary-generals getting their full maximum eight-year run!

This guy is a record holder of record holders—elected five times in a political system whose electoral integrity may not be close to Platonic but is probably no worse than that of America's Chicago in the not-so-distant past.

But hardly anyone in the West knew (or knows) who he is, or what they missed, or what—with a little give-and-take on both sides, including and perhaps especially from him—this manipulative political genius might have meant in helping the West to smooth some of the troubled waters over the ever-roiling clash of Islamic-versus-Western civilizations.

There's a major tragedy here that's not immediately obvious.

But it is the obvious that ultimately takes us in the direction that solves the mystery of Mahathir. I think you will see what I mean. Just come along with me on this trip into the mind of quite possibly the most successful mainstream Muslim politician of our time.

ALL of our interviews are to take place in the former PM's office in either Putrajaya or Petronas Tower One. I had wanted them to be in a less formal setting, but Dr M felt he didn't have the time for that. It was as if, now being out of office, he only wanted to be interviewed in an office.

He might even feel more secure in an office—any office. After all, over the years Western journalism has depicted him, variously, as an anti-Semite, a racist, a jerk, an ignoramus.

But has the depiction been fair? Who is the real Dr Mahathir? Why not let him tell us himself?

After all, Dr M, at his truest, is not one for holding back. He is a political master of almost everything except understatement. But he is not all talk. He is a big-time doer. In fact, we are using 'James Bond' movie titles (or variations thereof) as chapter headings because there's a part to Dr Mahathir that's all action—and so we make him out to be more like a *Dr Yes* than a *Dr No*. Nothing better illustrates the former Can-Do *Dr Yes* of modernizing Malaysia than the sight of the two Petronas Towers, at the time of their erection the world's tallest towers.

Asia is such a competitive freak these days, both within itself as well as outside of itself. It seems as if whatever one country must do, another will try to do it better—or at least something or other in response. Dr Mahathir, when he was prime minister, was notorious for the edificial overstatement.

This was boisterous braggadocio design and careering ambition at its least apologetic. The point of it all? Before then, who would have believed such backbreaking effort would be even possible in otherwise super laid-back Malaysia?

Yet that, of course, was precisely the point. The good doctor's diagnosis of the Malay malady was related to its diagnosed inferiority complex and excessive mellowness. And so the remedy would be to concoct some inescapable symbol of Malaysia standing up for itself and showing the world it could reach heights as high as almost anybody. He understood the need of the repressed Asian ego to reach for the skies—and its destiny—in a collective cry for overdue recognition.

I AM more than ready for my Dr M close-up.

It is a sweltering September morning in downtown Kuala Lumpur. The vast lobby of the Petronas Towers complex is filled with office workers, shoppers and a good tumble of tourists jammed into the standard-office-building oval lobby that connects Tower One with Tower Two.

I make my way toward the tower that houses the KL office of former PM Mahathir. That would be in Tower One—but of course it would be one, not two. On the 86th floor would be his office.

A long line is waiting for a tour, which includes the breathtaking skybridge on the 41st floor connecting the towers. My appointment is ten minutes away and the line looks ten hours long. Have I miscalculated?

From out of nowhere a security guard zooms toward me. He is friendly—and highly informed. "You are Professor Plate," he says, referring to my academic title. He smiles and points to the elevator bank. We wade through a crowd. He rides up with me. We transfer to another elevator bank and he leaves me at Reception Desk outside the 86th floor office.

The trip to the top took like three minutes. I don't remember New York's World Trade Center elevators ever working this smoothly. Back then it seemed you'd be like clanking floor by grudging floor toward maybe Mt Everest on a slow day. Of course the Manhattan monsters came decades before Petronas. This joint is presumably state-of-the-art edifice-complex engineering. I wonder how much Dr M micro-managed it when he was PM.

The former prime minister stands up and smiles, we shake hands, and I start arraying my two baby digital video cameras around him from various points on his oak desk. He starts laughing a little as one camera falls off its tripod and I drop another on the floor.

"I know, you're seeing amateur hour here."

He tells me I can't balance the left camera on a pile of books: "What are you trying to do?" he says, not gruffly... almost in a genial tone.

"I'm trying to record you. This is camera number two," I explain, referring to the one I can't get to sit up straight.

He says: "This is linked to the CIA?"

"What?" I'm barely half-listening, annoyed with myself for having so much trouble getting a simple camera not much bigger than a candy bar to stand upright.

"Yes," I say, staring at him, getting the half-joke finally. "Direct to video screens in Langley, Virginia."

This is his sometimes-perky off-the-wall sense of humor. He likes to push at boundaries just to see what might happen.

He smiles.

Finally finished with fiddling and arranging my Flipshare HD mini-cameras, I sit down, too. The first interview is to begin.

CAN we get this guy figured out right? This is the point often missed with this extraordinary politician: in many ways, during the 22 years of his prime ministry, Dr Mahathir Mohamad was arguably the world's single most important practicing Muslim national political leader.

Jews may think he is their enemy, and maybe they are right. But in my view they have got it wrong—tragically wrong. And in no little measure this is what this small book is about.

Look at the matter this way.

Through his 22 years in power, through five elections, there's something electrically opposite about Muslim terrorists and Mahathir the Muslim. They come from the same world—the Islamic world—and yet it is as if they are from different planets.

Isn't it interesting that for the 22 years the former family physician served as head of his party and as prime minister, Malaysia suffered not a single terrorist incident?

And it has a 62-percent-or-so Muslim population.

And its long-dominant political party, the United Malays National Organization (UMNO), is Malay-run.

And it has a pure-bred religious-driven party (comprised in some proportion of so-called 'ultras', radical Muslims), known as PAS (Parti Islam se-Malaysia, or Pan-Malaysian Islamic Party), which at any moment might have tried to seize power in the northern conservative states of Kelantan and Terengganu where they have a strong (and to some, terrifying) foothold.

But you witnessed no nightclubs blowing up, like in Muslim Indonesia, where tourists had their lives cruelly ended. No car bombs erupting in the parking garages of hotels. No ethnic bloodshed spilled over onto the streets. By and large, Malaysia was calm and collected—and Muslim to the core.

Success has many fathers but failure—goes the familiar saying—is almost always an orphan. To be sure, there are all sorts of explanations for those 22 years of Malaysian harmony. One could credit the fact that Malaysia's Muslims mainly hail from the relatively mellow Sunni sect, unlike in other Muslim countries (such as Iraq), where, say, Sunnis and Shias are constantly at each other's throats.

Or one could simply credit the argument that the Malay-Muslims of Malaysia are somehow a milder and more moderate personality than Muslims in other countries because, well, over the years they have behaved more moderately and more mildly.

You get the picture. That's no explanation. It's the sun is hot because the sun is hot.

Here's our point: almost everyone and everything gets credit for more than two decades of racial and religious harmony—except the one man who actually ran the country for those two decades plus. There's a side to Mahathir which, forgetting about all the bombast, most people don't notice. It's a wonder why. Then again—perhaps it isn't.

I re-start this way, not dishonestly, expressing tourist-level admiration for the formidable Petronas Towers project, with its view-to-thrill payoff, and suggesting that this was one government project that did not get messed up.

I throw this out: "Aides can sometimes tell you one thing and then do something else."

He grimaces as if swallowing a live rat.

"Like that old British television series 'Yes, Minister', where the underlings always agreed with everything the top dog wants to do, except somehow nothing ever gets done."

He hadn't watched the legendary series but quickly got the idea. Getting the gist of an idea from whatever source comes naturally to him, I was to discover.

"Yeah."

I wait and do nothing—often a tactic of mine when interviewing the functional but stalling egomaniacs I tend to run across.

Then him saying: "But I take a very big role. I actually go down to see these projects."

"Don't you have lieutenants who do that, or a combination of both ... or how does that work?"

He looks a little impatient with me but not at all put out: "I visit work sites. Perhaps more often than the contractors themselves [*we laugh at that*]... I talk to the engineers in charge."

"Like with the Petronas project?

"Yeah, Petronas. I would come to Petronas [construction site] almost every week."

I chime in: "Actually, I shouldn't say thus perhaps, but the World Trade Center, which I'd been into many times before it went down ... umm, I think yours is better-built. I mean, it just gives you a much better feeling. Do you have to get in the details of, like ... I mean, do you know things about construction normal people don't?"

"Perhaps I know more—"

"So that you're not fooled?"

"… about things that I'm involved with than most people who are in my position."

"Why?"

He sighs: "If I make a decision, I want to know more or less how it should be implemented."

"Right."

"Because I have always believed that, uh, it's no good just making decisions. You need to follow up your decision by ensuring that it's being carried out."

There is a bit of an awkward pause. Malaysia is rather infamous—though anything but unique—for inefficient government. It suffers by comparison with neighboring Singapore. There, Lee Kuan Yew and his successors have installed a level of government that on its best days rivals a Honda factory careering for the monthly productivity award … which almost every month it wins.

Dr Mahathir is well aware of his country's reputation for comic governance. He knows what he inherited when he first became PM in 1981. He remains in a measure of denial: "You know, I changed the practice in the government. In the past, the cabinet makes the decisions, and then there is a one-line instruction going to the ministries."

"Mhm." I don't want to quarrel this early in our conversations; and probably with 10,000 workaholic Mahathirs in the right bureaucratic spots, the Malaysian government might crack it into the big leagues of Top Ten All-World Governments. But...

"This is the cabinet's decision."

"Right." But do they listen or care?

He answers: "And they have to figure out how to go about carrying out the decision."

I detect a touch of skepticism on his face. Or maybe I am reading into his.

He shrugs, shrugs again: "Sometimes they don't even know how to do it! And then, they won't understand the decision."

Which means the cabinet has been talking to itself, in effect.

"Or they may think that the decision was all wrong, because they cannot understand it. And, uh, then of course they tend to formulate their own, uh, interpretation, which actually has been debated in the cabinet..."

"Right."

He looks up, into the distance, as if trying to find some reality to focus on: "...an interpretation that we have rejected for whatever reason. But, after I noticed that they were not able to understand, I immediately ordered that, after the cabinet meeting, all ministers are to meet their senior officers, and explain to them what is the decision of the cabinet and why that decision is made, and how it is going to be carried out."

What he is trying to say, it seems to me, is he had a lot of struggles with the Malaysian bureaucracy. Well, at least Malaysia's not India...

I put in: "Right, because from the top down, it filters down, it gets messed up a lot."

"Yeah, it gets interpreted in different ways."

Me chiming in: "Sometimes willfully, and sometimes it just happens."

"Because it's just the nature of human beings. That's why I also believe that if you make a decision, you must know something about how to implement the decision."

"Really? That puts you into the position of almost micro-managing."

He nods, not denying that: "So I insisted that ministers go down and see to the implementation because there may be snags, and the officers concerned are not able to solve this because this is cabinet decision, and they cannot change it. So, when the ministers are there, on the scene, they can see that these are impossible things, and maybe the minister needs to go back to the cabinet, maybe he needs to propose that it be modified."

"Mhm ... it sounds like a formula for an endless cycle of appeals and re-appeals."

He shakes his head, and waves the idea off: "No, that is alright, because minor modification is okay. But, if it's a major change, it has to go to the minister who has access to the cabinet."

"And that's where the revised decision can be made."

"The relevant minister can, at the next cabinet meeting, say, 'Look, you made this decision, but it is just impossible to implement.' "

"Right."

"He can say, 'We need to change; we need to modify it so that it is implementable.' "

"Right. You would accept that as a response, but what you won't accept is, uh, nothing happens."

"Yeah."

Honestly, he seemed darn proud of this.

Perhaps not a lot of Malaysians will find Mahathir's boast about cabinet reform in Malaysia wholly convincing.

But there's some evidence that he did help push things in a better direction. It was no surprise when the corruption rating from Transparency International, the well-respected European nonprofit watchdog that praises clean government, offered his country a lowly rating of 56th in the world in its most recent assessment. This put it behind even Jordan, though ahead of Cuba! After leaving office, Mahathir himself has been untouched by prosecutors, but not all his aides: a top-ranking former Perwaji steel executive was fingered for corruption. (For the record, the rating winners were New Zealand, Denmark and Singapore.)

But Malaysia did a lot better in another category. The equally well-respected World Competitive Yearbook annual, from the prestigious Swiss business school IMD, ranks the pro-business atmosphere of countries around the world. Again, Singapore finished in the top three—ahead of the U.S. and Hong Kong, in fact. But Malaysia finished in the top ten in the world—not bad at all.

Perhaps Malaysia's image for government efficiency is behind the reality. Maybe part of Malaysia's image problem is that it's in a tough competitive neighborhood. Singapore, that annoying neighbor to the south, consistently finishes near the top or at the top of so many good-government lists. If it could just get Singapore to relocate to a different continent, Malaysia might not look so bad at all.

A Mahathir Political Point
Serious bad will start to pile up in your government when after a cabinet meeting, nothing happens. Nothing happening is not progress. Sometimes you just have to do it yourself.

Live and Let Worship

**The Gore blunder ... Islamic extremism
... no moderate Muslim ... I am *not* an ultra!**

FOR years Malaysia has been no menace to any other country
(leaving aside the silly bickering with Singapore). And internally
its race and ethnic relations became, on the global scale, a relative
model of mildness. To the credit of Mahathir and other committed
Malaysians, the country avoided the extreme behaviors that seemed
to spring up elsewhere. However one might define the term,
taking in as many factors as you want, Malaysia, with more than
60 percent of its population Muslim, has to be tabbed as an icon of
the so-called moderate Muslim state.

That's why it is sad that not enough of us Americans are
aware of even where it should be located on the terror/moderation
map ... or even where it is on *any* map. But the nation and its
people attracted greater attention after the catastrophic suicide
bombings of the twin World Trade Center Towers in 2001. For in
the weeks and months after that, Washington scrambled to figure
out which governments in the Islamic world were against it—and
which were not; and which could be related to easily, and which
could not.

It was a simplistic, Manichean calibration, and the positioning of the Mahathir government on the worldwide Islamic terrorist map was internationally transparent. Kuala Lumpur was part of the solution, not part of the problem.

The fact of the matter is that Mahathir's internal-security police were all over their own resident—and even visiting—extremists like night-crawlers at low tide. Whatever the trouble-makers were hoping to do elsewhere or planning to do elsewhere, what they were permitted to do, on Malaysian soil at least, could be summed up in one word: nothing. There was a 24/7 surveillance and infiltration lockdown. And Dr M did not believe in complete freedom of public political expression, if it turned out to be too costly.

The irony of course was the almost overnight change in Mahathir's image. It went—at least in Washington's eyes—from political bone-crusher to Islamic-extremist lion-tamer. Until then, Malaysia had been a perennial negative poster-boy in the Western human rights hall of shame.

The Mahathir government had come under constant Western criticism for many years before 2001. The country was cited for all sorts of inadequacies and anti-democratic apostasies, including political repression, crony capitalism and judicial corruption. (A great deal of the unrelenting criticism came from the West. But in recent years Mahathir's second successor, Dato' Sri Najib Tun Razak, has received some praise for lifting some restrictions on freedom of expression and the media. Still, a tidal change is not evident yet.)

And until 2001, in fact, it sometimes seemed that almost everyone in the world knew how best to manage Malaysia and its Muslims better than the one man who had been doing so for almost two decades. Even the Clinton administration, which by its second term was rounding into a responsible adult administration (more or less) and should have known better, got into the act of proposing to another government how it should conduct its affairs. That country was Malaysia.

In 1998 it attacked Mahathir on his home soil, no less. The judge and jury was none other than Al Gore, standing in for President Bill Clinton in Malaysia at the Asia Pacific Economic Cooperation (APEC) summit. In his speech, Gore, serving in effect as a knee-jerk global lobbyist for the West's human rights crowd, lambasted the Mahathir government for its arrest, ill treatment and continued prosecution of Anwar Ibrahim, until then the deputy prime minister.

Gore did raise fair issues. And Dr Mahathir did not help Malaysia's image by leaving his suddenly dumped number-two to the tender mercies of his police, who arrested him on various charges (including sodomy) and badly mistreated him in prison. Surely, the obvious lessons of 1987's Operation Lalang would have indicated a more judicious course of action (see "The Men With the Golden Guns" on pages 114–126). But Gore turned what would have been a winning issue for the West into a losing one by attacking Dr M right in his own Malaysia.

No one likes it when a guest comes into their home and offers unwanted criticism. Even when the U.S. has a fair point to make, it defeats its purpose by lecturing people in public and, worse yet, on their turf. Rudeness is rarely effective. What's more, the U.S. does not exactly own a perfect human rights record.

Worse yet, the Gore attack, in a hotel ballroom in Kuala Lumpur, had the unintended consequence of hurting Anwar and helping Mahathir. With one arrogant America-knows-best blowhard speech, the United States metamorphosed from saint (on the side of liberalization) to bully (lecturing foreigners on how to run their country). As is often the case, we blow it when we blow our own horn obnoxiously, in someone's own backyard.

History's perspective doesn't make Gore or the Clinton administration look much better.

Consider that just a few years later, when 9/11 exploded on the scene, the West was all a-scramble to establish relationships with 'sensible, moderate' Muslim governments. Guess who—symbolically speaking—was suddenly being invited to dinner, as we say in the U.S.? It was none other than Mr Moderate Muslim himself.

What does the (oh-so-suddenly) wonderful, all-knowing and wise Dr M know about these seriously demented and dangerous Islamic terrorists groups, and how has he so skillfully contained them over the years?

In truth, Mahathir's firm-handed management of potential Islamic extremist cells was no overnight phenomenon in elite U.S. security circles. He was well known to, and much appreciated by, the U.S. military. For the Asia-Pacific region, its headquarters is at Camp Smith near Pearl Harbor, Hawaii. The U.S. Pacific Command (PACOM) had strong ties to the Malaysian military (though the Malaysian brass, interestingly enough, was largely educated at Great Britain's famous Sandhurst, not the U.S.'s West Point. Even so, the Malaysian-U.S. military relationship was always stronger than generally realized.).

All this was running through my head rapidly as I ask Dr M in his office at Petronas Towers: "Now, at one point, perhaps many NGOs and so forth in the West thought that your government's repression of some of these elements was, uh, terrible and so awful and so forth. But then after 9/11, the West realized that some of the people you were dealing with were very tough and dangerous characters who would blow up a Petronas Tower if they had a chance, right?"

He averts my look on that point but who could doubt it? The nihilistic and militaristic strategy of extremist Islam is both a continuing reality and a true embarrassment to all sensible people, Muslim or not.

I continue: "Umm, how did you do that? How did you work it? You had 24 million people of which maybe 100,000 or whatever were actually or potentially dangerous. Well, how did you do it? Did you have to develop new methods of surveillance, infiltration —I know you don't want to give away state secrets, but—and did the FBI say, after 9/11, come to you and say, 'We see you in a different way, now. Tell us your tricks.' "

"Yeah, I think, firstly, this idea that I'm a moderate Muslim ... that is false."

"It's not true?" (If I sound greatly surprised here, I greatly am.)

"I'm not."

"You're not?"

"I am a Muslim fundamentalist."

"Okay, okay." I say okay, but I don't mean okay.

Dr M continues: "I tell people that, because if you follow the true teachings as found in the Quran and the verified traditions of the Prophet, you will become a very good man. You don't want to have enemies, you don't want to fight with people—you defend yourself, yes—but you need not be aggressive. These are the teachings."

I nod and say nothing. But this is his long-held view. It even extends to his view on national defense budgets: they should cost no more than one percent of a country's annual income.

He continues: "But over 1,400 years of Islam, there have been many interpreters of Islam, and each one of them is influenced by the needs of the moment. They explain that their acts of terror and violence are due to Islam. *It's not, you know! Islam doesn't teach you to do that.* So I get guided by that, and Islam demands that I be fair. That, to a Muslim, is what it says in the Quran—to you, your religion; to me, my religion. You pray in your own way; I pray in my own way. And there is no compulsion in religion. So, I adhere to that teaching—become a Muslim fundamentalist, and Muslim fundamentalism must let me be moderate. You see?"

Let us review that invaluable sentence again, repeat it for time immemorial … and may everyone (Muslim and not) listen up: *Muslim fundamentalism must let me be moderate.*

A Mahathir Political Point

Muslim fundamentalism must let me be moderate. Having accepted that, my dealings with the non-Muslims become very easy.

Dr M continues: "So, having accepted that, my dealings with the non-Muslims become very easy. If I seem to be favoring [any one group of] them too much, that would be wrong. I have to be moderate. That's the teaching of my religion, and I must be moderate. Our religion forbids this, this instability, confusion and all that … you shouldn't create that. That is why I value, if there is any legacy that I leave behind, it is the fact that, during my time, there were no racial clashes."

It is redundant for me to say this but I say it anyway: "That's an important legacy."

Mahathir nods appreciatively and continues: "The Chinese who once hated me work well with me. The Indians work with me, and the Malays were quite happy with the way I treat the Chinese. They don't ask me to be extreme, you see? What is their right, I protect. What is the right of the non-Muslims, I protect. And the Chinese, they want to have a stable situation where they can do business."

"Yes, that's the famed Chinese pragmatism, alright."

"We provided that."

There's a lot of statistical evidence to back that up, and anecdotal support as well.

Me saying: "Right. So, if you're a true-to-the-Quran Muslim fundamentalist, nonetheless, in the area of statehood, you could be perceived accurately as somehow acting in moderation."

"Yeah."

"But to be a Muslim fundamentalist, that does not mean you're an ultra?"

An 'ultra', especially in Malaysia, is exactly what that sounds like—an extremist.

"No."

"But there are of course different schools of thought in Islam, as there was over the centuries in Christianity?"

"Yeah."

"And some were decidedly aggressive … the Crusades, the Jesuits, the Inquisition, and so on. And you have some of that in Islam, and some of that is supported financially by other powers that are Islamic and sitting on a ton of oil. Has that created, did that create problems of governance for you?"

He knows I am talking about Saudi Arabia, among others, and mulls that over by placing his hands on his huge desk and runs them, palms down, across the top like minesweepers: "You know, when I started, and when I was appointed deputy prime minister, and therefore I would be the next prime minister, the

Chinese community used to call me the Malay Ultra; that I was an extremist, and, uh, they were afraid of me. But throughout my 22 years, there were no racial clashes, and at the end of my 22 years, my strongest supporters were the Chinese."

"Because the Chinese like strength, don't they?"

"Yeah. And they want to do business. I mean, if you are always fair to them, I think they will be okay."

"Was there any time when it would have been fair to say that Mahathir was an ultra?"

"Why, no, it's not fair at all."

"Never, huh? Not even as a youth?"

"You know, in politics, one of the most effective ways of trying to kill your opponent is to give a label to him. You get called an ultra, you know, and everything that you do, which is very fair to everybody, will be labeled as extreme. You see, that's the importance of ultra [as a political label], and the word ultra was used [against me] by Lee Kuan Yew."

"Right. But you say you were never an ultra, even as a youth."

Dr M shakes his head.

I say: "But now with PAS, the Muslim religious party, do they have ultras in there?" Well of course they do, but we want to hear Dr M say it.

He tilts his head to one side: "Yeah, there are people there who are not realistic. They don't understand this country. They don't understand that this is a multiracial country; like it or not, you have to live together. You know, we can't get rid of the Chinese.

I used to tell the Malays, you know, get rid of the Chinese and all those buildings around, you will go to seed! [*laughs to himself*] That is absolutely true because the Chinese are the manufacturers, they are the movers and shakers; they're very tied-in people, we need them. We have to accept them. But they, on their side, they must also realize the needs of the indigenous people of Malaysia."

What he means here is acceptance of the government program to help the majority Malays with the kind of quotas and affirmative-action programs we in the States engineer for minorities. But that program—though partly successful—has also been controversial, creating in effect a culture of dependency among the majority Malays that has had the unintended consequence of rendering some of them less economically capable.

But Dr M stayed with that approach for his 22 years: "During my time, I had expressed this. I said, we need you [the Chinese minority], but you must also realize that you're in this country, and you need the [majority Malay] people here. You see, you take everything for yourself and leave nothing for them [the Malays], and what do they do? They might tie a bomb to their bodies and blow themselves up. That's bad."

Dr M doesn't expressly say it, here or in any of the interviews. But you know what he means: if the Malaysian government were to suspend affirmative action for the majority Malays, he would tend to predict the worst. Either short-term agitation or violence of some kind; or over the long run, the rise to ultimate power of the radical PAS party. And then the Chinese and the Indians would wind up paying a far higher bill than they pay under the current arrangement.

In other words, his programs for giving the majority some advantages in employment and educational opportunity cannot be judged simply on economic grounds.

A Mahathir Political Point

Starve people long enough and instead of dying they become dangerous. Governing them rationally can serve to remove the conditions under which irrational governance becomes truly dangerous.

I try to push him back to his moderate Muslim fundamental philosophy, which I find fascinating: "I think that part of the wisdom of Mahathir that's relevant to our time, and to the future, and a key part of your legacy, is yeah, you built great highways through Putrajaya and Kuala Lumpur, and developed the Langkawi resort, and the airport and towers and highways, and your government improved education and health—in some ways you're ahead of us in health policy—but I still think part of your magic has been helping manage all these different religious tensions."

As part of Southeast Asia, Malaysia wasn't a cauldron of just one strand of tension—say, Chinese versus Malay. All kinds of ethnic, religious and political tensions flow through one of the world's most populated regions like varying weather patterns. In

Mahathir's mind it is the job of the political boss man to sometimes stand up against political nature and try to change—in effect—the weather!

He says: "Well, all communities have got extremists, and unfortunately extremists have too much of an influence on the 'moderate' majority. If you say something against them, they say oh, you're not adhering to the teachings of our religion. This is a problem. See, we are allowing ourselves to be captive to the extremists in our own society. But to answer the extremists, you must be correct in your interpretation."

Mahathir sighs as if he has gone over this in his mind—and with some of his more 'action-oriented' people—again and again: "If they say, 'Well, they kill us, so we must kill them,' you can answer, 'Well, okay. You can kill them.' After you kill them, their people will kill you. After their people kill you, you kill them. In the end, what happens? Nothing ... you know? What is the sacrifice for? You're going to Heaven? Well, you don't know, you see, because Islam forbids killing of people. Then you justify it by saying they are the enemies, but you are not getting anything. So, if you argue [for non-violent understanding and coexistence] on the basis of the teachings of the religion, I think you will be alright, even with some extremists."

Dr M is speaking with obvious conviction, so I ask: "And in your view, an honest, sensible, commonsense reading of the Quran does lead to a cosmopolitan government that is respectful of vast differences, does not require missionary conversion, 9/11 and things like that … is that right? Or, are you just taking the Quran and bending it to the perspective of the sensible country doctor that you are."

He is emphatic: "Mm, *not*. You have to read. You know, the message sometimes comes indirectly. For example, the first message received by the Prophet was, Read, *Iqraq*, Read! And these people say, you read only religion, not anything else. But, if you look at the time when the message came to the Prophet, there was nothing to read other than Hebrew literature, other than the writings of the Greeks and all that. So, that is important, we have to learn about those things. But they missed the whole message by giving it an interpretation that reading is [only] about religion. So, a lot of the messages in the Quran get misinterpreted."

I chip in: "Right, because the Prophet presumably knew what was available to read at that time, and wasn't stupid, and therefore it's only a kind of very narrow reading to say you can only read a religious book. And, in fact for a period of time, in the evolution of our civilization, Muslim science and art was cutting-edge. Do you despair that it will ever be cutting-edge again, or do you think it's going to come back?"

Mahathir believes a thoroughly modern Islam is the only possible salvation of the Muslim religion and Islamic culture: "I think that there is a great deal more consciousness about the role of other fields of knowledge for the religious, now. For example, the religion says that Muslims must have the capacity to defend themselves, and it mentioned having warhorses. That was in the time of the Prophet. Today, if we have warhorses, we are not going to be able to defend ourselves. You need guns, you need tanks, you need battleships. To have them, you need to have knowledge of science. You see how, in a roundabout way, if you interpret it correctly, to defend means you have to have knowledge. That will cause you to study all these other fields of knowledge."

"Right, and if you talk to people like Singapore's well-known diplomat and educator Kishore Mahbubani for example. Kishore has been saying that the 21st century will showcase the rise of Asia—the Asian Century. Will that include a revitalized Islamic Asia?"

"I think it will not be an Islamic Asia, because obviously, the Chinese, the Japanese, the Koreans … they are way ahead. But the Muslims will be much better educated and adjusted to the situation around them. You see, the Asian civilization antedated the European civilization. China was civilized 4,000 years ago, when there were cavemen in Europe."

"Yeah I know, the Chinese want copyrights for everything."

Dr M's eyebrows shoot up and we both laugh.

He says: "See, so it's not something new that we need to be frightened of."

"Right, right. But do you see the evolution, of even a kind of energetic evolution, of Islam into modernity proceeding at a faster pace?"

"Yes, I think so."

But not all Islamic governments favor the new theology of modern Islam. I say: "But some resistance is supported financially by other powers who are Islamic and sitting on tons of oil. Even more oil than you have. Has that created problems of governance for you? How did you handle that?"

Mahathir slows down and takes a deep breath. This is a touchy one. He looks out the window, then back at me. He decides to answer by emphasizing how he sells modernity to Muslims who may be skeptical, or even critical:

"You know, when you're dealing with a problem [or an objection] that is somehow connected with religion, you cannot answer that problem [or quiet that objector] by doing something that is totally unrelated to religion. You have to give the religious explanation as to what you are doing. So, if you say, well, all we need to do is to develop this country and give the people a lot of money, income and a good life—for them, that's not important. What's important is, this is what Islam wants us to do, and if you are not doing it, then you are in the wrong."

"You have to go back to The Book."

"Yeah, go back to The Book. In Malay we say, 'When you are lost, go back to the beginning.' So, the beginning is the Quran. Because for 1,400 years, there have been numerous interpretations, and the interpretations are different, each from the other, so much so that they clash.

"You see Sunnis fighting against Shias and all that. That is not Islam. At the time of the Prophet, there were no Sunnis, no Shias. As much as at the time of Christ, there were no Protestants, there were no Calvinists, there were no, uh, none of these, uh, extreme what do you call it, people, uh ... fundamentalists. Christian fundamentalists."

He is talking faster now, stumbling no more: "All these things are not due to the religion, not due to Christianity. It is due to people who have some vested interest to interpret the religion for their own purpose, you see. Then, of course, they fight the other. They burn the other as heretics and things like that. It's not following the teachings of Christianity."

I interject: "Is the degree of internal clash within the Islamic civilization ... is it substantially self-destructive?"

"It is self-destructive, but fortunately in Malaysia, we come from one Sunni group. We are all followers of Shafie school, but we are very tolerant among ourselves. We have political differences, but not so much religious, although they try to make it a religious difference.

"But I have to point out to them that what they are saying is wrong *in the religion*. I'm not saying that it is wrong because it is not going to help us develop this country. That is not an answer for them. But I have to tell them why their interpretation is wrong, and I have to back it up."

A Mahathir Political Point
**The governance of a polity that has a
predominant religious core cannot safely
proceed on purely secular grounds.**

I try to rephrase it this way: "If you have an objection from the Muslim community that's based on religion, you can't answer it solely in terms of governance issues, or policy issues; you need to respond in terms of religious answers, right? Okay. That to me says that if a country has any significant percentage of Muslims, at the very highest level you have to have someone who both understands the government and understands the religion, otherwise you're going to have misgovernment. Right?"

Mahathir nods emphatically. Obviously, he is not proposing to advise Turkey on how to govern itself. It is a far older nation with a much different history that spans centuries, with an official determination to secularize its governance and leave behind its Islamic Ottoman past. Unlike Malaysia, though, Turkey's secular governance has had to endure many coups and continues to face serious unrest.

"My wife Andrea—who, as she puts it, is a 'fallen' Jew—asked about this religious dimension to modern governance, and I told her that my sense of the Mahathir touch is, if PAS—the religious radicals or the purists or whatever—if they got a hold of an issue, whether it was on, say, skirt length or beer drinking by a woman at a hotel bar, or whatever it is—Mahathir would not let them monopolize that issue.

"He would slice into that issue and take some of it away from them, so they couldn't push out on it and leverage it out, even though if in his heart in a different time and a different place he would say, 'What the hell, what do I care if a woman has a beer at a hotel bar' … but he was loathe to permit the purists to monopolize the issue and make it their own and thus increase their political space. Is that close to accurate?"

He smiles at my effort to simplify, but knows he has to add this: "Yeah … but this development should never crop up because if [as the leader] I command on this sort of issue, I command on the basis of the religion. I don't say that in modern times you don't do this kind of thing, this is out of date, and that. This is their interpretation of religion, which gets them into this kind of situation."

A Mahathir Political Point

The way to permit extremists to appear reasonable is for the non-extremists to give up too much ground by reverting to secular standards of reason.

So the secular leader's decision in a largely Muslim society has to be grounded in religious reason; otherwise, you see, it's in effect unreasonable. But such decision-making doesn't have to be by draconian Islamic decree. Making religious decisions as leader of a country doesn't mean the effect of the decisions has to be, by modern secular standards, brutal. The Prophet, like Christ, was always merciful.

But the Islam we in the West, through our media, see most often is the harsh version. So I say: "Right, but some of these people are not merciful. Yet you can't look too soft, right? Because, then they get more space and more prominence, right?"

He sighs and almost glances at his watch, as if a Western psychiatrist hoping the intense session might soon be over so he can have some release.

I understand this has been an emotionally tough line of conversation, so I say: "Very last question this session. In the Islamic world, today, who would you say are the outstanding progressive thinkers and leaders, people whom you admire, either for the quality of their theological thinking, their cosmopolitanism or whatever?"

The question re-engages his flagging attention, and his direct and profound answer almost takes my breath away.

He says, standing up: "There are some people, but they are not allowed to surface because the orthodox thinking is very powerful."

"The *what* thinking?"

"Orthodox."

"I see."

"They are very powerful. So, these people will never appear, well, to be anybody at all. They are crushed before they can surface, so it's very difficult to identify them."

It's easy to see why Dr M does not want to be identified as a moderate Muslim. Because, as a putative *fundamentalist* Muslim, he can stake out a position that makes any deviation from the basic canon seem extremist. By contrast, a *moderate* Muslim position might appear wimpy and leave too much political space for extremely non-moderate True Believers to seize control.

This session was especially intense, but well worth it.

Who else other than a real-world, street-smart but highly educated man like Mahathir can hope to outmaneuver those elements of Islam most feared by the West?

Neither of us has any gas left to keep us going another kilometer.

From a side jacket pocket I pull out my digital camera and say, in the decisive announcement-tone of the first guest at a dinner party announcing it's time to leave: "Alright. Do you have anyone on your staff here who can take some pictures of two gorgeous, middle-aged men?"

That cuts the tension.

Says Dr M: "Middle-aged?!!"

Dr Mahathir Defines His Muslim Religion

After all the conversations were done, I faxed from my home in Los Angeles a few questions for clarification. Here were Dr Mahathir's responses, faxed back from his Putrajaya office and personally signed.

TP: Muslimism is in no respect in conflict at all with your philosophy. • **Dr M:** I adhere to the fundamental teachings of Islam as founded in the Quran and the verified traditions of the Prophet.

TP: Ataturk, though a secularist, was an ethnic cleanser to achieve his goal of the secular Turkish state; you, though an Islamicist, believe in a secular government for all and are by stark contrast a let's-all-live-together multiculturalist. • **Dr M:** Yes.

TP: The Shah of Iran, before his fall, could be described as a secularizing and modernizing autocrat; you are properly described as a Muslim modernizer. • **Dr M:** Yes.

TP: You believe Islam need not be an insurmountable obstacle to progress, but an overly literal Quranic Islam can be. • **Dr M:** Yes.

TP: For the thoroughly modern Mahathir, Internet technology is not the enemy but an asset. It can help draw together the umma [the whole community of Muslims bound together by ties of religion] with the savvy Muslim Malaysia perhaps taking the lead. • **Dr M:** Yes.

TP: The deprioritization of individual wants and ego comes up in the Asian values discussion, but this is in particular emphasized in Islam. • **Dr M:** Yes.

TP: Your Mahathirism adheres to the early 'instructional' meaning of the Quran, not the later 'al-Qaeda' meaning. • **Dr M:** Yes.

TP: It is correct to term you a 'Muslim pacifist', without unilateral disarmament, of course. • **Dr M:** Yes.

TP: You forswear the term 'moderate Muslim', which won't be used in this book but we can use the term 'mainstream Muslim'. • **Dr M:** Not mainstream Islam which often differs from the fundamental teaching of Islam as found in the Quran, but fundamental Islam before being subjected to personal and differing interpretations by the learned ones and by those who wish to justify their agenda through misinterpretations.

Goldenguy

**Medical woes ... Argentinean horseman
... Lee Kuan Yew ... the Singapore Protocol**

DR M often describes himself as a born politician who early on
became a doctor out of necessity, and then found his way into what
Allah really intended for him to be—a politician.

I am nestled in front of his big, rounded glass desk. Beneath is
a ravishing dark blue deep-set carpet, and out the windows to his
back are vast vistas of downtown Kuala Lumpur and, because we are
near the top of Petronas Tower One, the metropolitan area beyond.
Kuala Lumpur is notorious for air so thick it seems touchable. But
today, a bright September late morning, it is a clear day and you
can almost see forever.

"You went to medical school?"

He sighs. He's answered this question a thousand times. But
in this case there's a reason for my repetition. "Yeah." It was King
Edward VII College of Medicine—in Singapore.

"Are there medical schools here in Malaysia now?" There
weren't back then.

"Now there are many."

"And they're good?"

"Yeah, they're good. The med students qualify here, then they go abroad for their specialist training, though some of them train locally." There's a trace of pride in his voice.

"So they go to the usual places in the West?"

"Yes. They go. They go to America…" Then his mind, which you feel is shimmering in a thousand directions at once sometimes, goes random: "I had my operation by a local doctor, you know. I didn't go abroad."

"And you had a what … a bypass?"

Dr M takes a deep breath. Most older people tend to enjoy regurgitating their medical woes. At first it looks as if we may have another one here: "Yeah, 64. Well 1989, yeah I was 64. I had a heart attack and Malaysian doctors diagnosed it as an infarction, and they said I need to have a bypass. So, they asked me whether I wanted to go to America, to the Mayo Clinic or whatever, but I asked them whether they could do it, and they said they can but usually VIPs go to America. I said I didn't mind if I can be treated here, because if I had no confidence in my own people, how can I expect other people to have confidence in them?"

"Were you making a political decision and not a medical one?"

He stops to think then laughs: "Yeah I was making a political decision."

"A life or death political decision?"

Funny, eh? Just a little maybe?

He responds: "Yeah, but the doctors were good, too, I think."

I shot him a glance, and recall for him a funny story attributed to the late Ronald Reagan as he was being whisked to the hospital after the 1981 assassination attempt: "Do you remember when Reagan was shot and he was taken to the hospital? Remember what he said?"

Mahathir says nothing, just stares.

I continue: "Something like, 'I just hope the surgeon is a Republican!'"

We both laugh at that. Ol' Ron, always good for a laugh…

Dr M continuing: "Well, I didn't ask any questions, but I know the surgeon. He's the son of somebody I know very well, and yeah they're very good people, very skillful people."

"And your health since then has been good?"

"Yes, and I—normally after ten years you have to have a re-do, but I lasted 16 years and I began to have problems again, and I decided I will go for a second operation, which will be a much more difficult operation because of scar tissues—and again, I had the same doctor that tended to me."

"And it was ten years after? When was it?"

"It was 16 years after. Uh, I did this in 2007. Three years ago."

"Wow. You're still so sharp. Do you feel like you're in your eighties?"

"Well I don't feel it."

He doesn't look it, either.

"Lots of people ask me, 'How do you keep young?' I say you choose your parents properly."

"You choose your *what?*"

"Choose your parents carefully."

We both laugh. It's probably a time-worn joke, but it was new to me.

Dr M obviously isn't the retiring type. It's hard to imagine him tooling around some senior citizens' nine-hole golf course in green-and-pink plaid pants. You gotta love that.

"You don't play golf, do you?"

"No, I don't play golf."

This makes me happy, confirms my sense of who he is: "See, I have a theory that golf is highly correlated with death among older people, as with retirement. So, if you avoid retirement, and you avoid golf, you have a chance at living a long life."

"Yeah."

"Well, you stay very active. I mean, you're in the papers every other day."

"I used to tell people that the most dangerous place is the bed because more people die in bed than anywhere else. [*we laugh*] I ride horses."

"Do you? I did not know that."

"I go to Argentina and I ride into the mountains."

"You go *where?*"

"Argentina. I go right up to the Chilean border."

"I did not know that. That's been a lifelong hobby?"

"Yeah. I learned to ride at the age of 60."

"Wow! That was when you were in office. You know, I asked

LKY that, what did you do to relieve stress? For example, Richard Nixon drank. No one's perfect, he drank. Some people yell and scream and have a terrible temper."

He considers that, then says: "I don't drink, I don't yell at people. I don't feel stressed, but obviously there must have been some stress. But I don't feel … I don't get excited. I don't get angry with people. People who work with me have been with me for more than 30 years."

"Is that right?"

"Yes. I believe that if you change your staff, you're going to deal with a newcomer and you have the problem of adjusting to him."

That can be tricky, though: "You have to be careful. From the first time you hire someone, you have to be really pretty sure."

"I mostly get along with people."

But that's not quite the point. It's possible to get along with someone who's incompetent, and not get along with the competent. If you never fire anybody (or almost never) you had better be a brilliant judge of talent from the get-go.

ONE person he decidedly does not get along with is Lee Kuan Yew, the ultra-competent founder of modern Singapore, who served for more than three decades (1959–90) as the island city's prime minister. Mahathir started later (1981) and finished up later (2003) but for residents of the Malay Peninsula, it seemed like they were always in each other's face.

For the decades of the 80s and 90s, these two Southeast Asian countries—one roughly the size and population of Los Angeles, the other roughly the size and population of California—were both led (and sometimes seemingly horsewhipped) by these two dynamic, unrelenting mega-personalities. Through their respective vision, energy, political style and combative grit, they not only propelled their nations up the arduous global economic ladder but also, almost by force of personality alone, stamped their countries with a high-profile identity.

They became the brand names of their respective countries.

But the fun part—at least for us outside observers—is that they seemingly could not stand the sight of each other. They quarreled in public, trash-talked about each other in private, and generally carried on like two divas unwilling to share the same stage.

The sprawling Malay Peninsula was barely big enough to contain them. In fact, during the ill-fated 1963-65 Federation of Malaysia period, when Singapore was part of the larger nation of Malaysia comprising Malaya, Sabah and Sarawak, they fought constantly in parliament in Kuala Lumpur. In the end the Malay elite decided to kick Lee out. Forced to leave and set up Singapore as a nation on its own, Lee was not sure that a city-state so tiny and frail could survive.

For their part, Mahathir and others at the highest political levels in Kuala Lumpur were certain only that they couldn't stand having the unsparingly brilliant—and relentlessly ambitious—Lee trying to fit into the same political space.

Mahathir versus Lee—what a power match-up! Like a pair of world-famous prize-fighting heavyweights. Two gunslingers convinced the tiny town wasn't big enough for both of them.

At the top of their games the two of them were so different— and yet so alike. They were both loved—and hated. They both had egos the symbolic equivalent of the two Petronas Towers themselves!

Mahathir has never made any secret of his dislike of Lee. He regards him as an over-the-top, overly ambitious Chinese would-be post-modern neo-emperor who couldn't be trusted. Many times he had said that or something like it, occasionally even in public.

However, like two peas in the proverbial pod, Mahathir and Lee have much in common.

Both seem to relish making painful decisions, work out almost daily for their health, profess similar social-Darwinian views, welcome outside multinational investment (while watching over outsiders like hawks), stoutly defend Asian values, view cultural factors as history's heavyweight players, and are ambivalent about increasing the size of the state (though untrusting of the free market to solve all social problems).

They often lecture their countrymen like schoolmarms, prioritize education, champion a sweltering, non-stop work ethic, warn against complacency, revere their mothers, married once and never divorced, are in awe of Israeli national achievements, and utterly detest golf, the slowest and most masochistic waste of time in the world.

Though hugging the bottom of the Malay Peninsula, and at this point configured in large part almost like a bloated exclamation point, Singapore and Malaysia in many ways could not be less alike.

Small and determined, the dot that is Singapore is multiracial but noisily Chinese, a whirling secular metropolis of go-go global ambition; above it, as it were, sits the greater portion of larger and much more laid-back Malaysia—multiracial but tonally Muslim and Malay, with a sprawling countryside that sometimes seems to anesthetize human energies and edginess with its natural beauty, wonder and even splendiferous smells, like one big natural valium.

But they did have one obvious and wholly significant thing in common besides geographical contiguity: political philosophy.

Like LKY, Dr M does not wish to be associated with two kinds of governments in particular. One is the inept kind that cannot remotely govern even its own affairs properly; the other is the kind of obnoxious government that wants to manage every other country's affairs.

They share the view that the system of American-style democracy won't work in many places, despite what they believe we Americans tend to think. (We Americans would have to admit that we sometimes do give out that impression.)

Me asking: "On the issue that you raised earlier, which is, we Americans have the silly notion that simply because the system of divided powers—democracy, 'one man, one vote'—in reality worked for us, therefore it has to work for everybody. You have raised a serious issue about that and so has LKY, so you agree with him in a way on that issue, don't you?"

"Yeah…"

He doesn't sound very happy about that unofficial accord, but yet proceeds: "The idea that all countries should be ruled in the same way, with the same system, to the same degree—you [Americans] are thinking about the impossible. People are different, because they are different."

There are not many patriotic American journalists who will admit to agreeing with this view. But—for worse or for better—I am one.

Dr M continuing: "You see, each person belongs to a particular race, not simply because he has the features of that particular race, but because he has the values that are upheld by that race. But to force him to discard his values, and accept a value that is foreign to him, I think it's not correct. It's wrong."

"Not going to work?"

"Worse is when you say, 'I will use force on you. I will have a regime change.' Even if you change the regime, it's not going to work. You look at what happened in Iraq. Okay, so they have forced Iraq to have a new government through killing a whole lot of people, but are you satisfied that Iraq is now a democracy?"

"Your good friend Lee Kuan Yew in Singapore once said, 'Maybe in a hundred years.' "

"In Iraq, he meant?"

I nod.

Mahathir has the look on his face of someone who is hating having to agree, but then admits, well, you have to hand it to that Singapore egomaniac, he got that one right.

"For Iraq, he shares your view," I say, having interviewed the legend of Singapore on that point before. "He says that each country starts in a different place, has different needs. I mean, you're going to hate this book because he's more like you than you realize!"

That thought makes us both chuckle.

"But are you really more of a democrat than he? I mean, aren't you both kind of semi-democrats at best?"

Dr Mahathir laughs as hard as he has all morning: "He's not democratic at all! You see, he goes through the formalities, but if there are any opposition politicians elected, he makes sure that they will be incapacitated, either by suing them for what they said during the election, and the suits will be settled with huge payments, compensation and all that; or the opposition will come in and be very quiet and not say anything.

"In Malaysia, we have always had opposition politicians, and they are very vocal ... *very* vocal. Of course, if they step beyond the limits, like trying to raise racial tension and all that, the government will have to act, but otherwise they are free, and in Malaysia [at times], five states out of the 13 states—five states!—[have been] under opposition rule, and in Parliament we have never been without a very vocal opposition."

He continues: "You see, because I myself believe that we

need the opposition. We need the opposition because otherwise we would not know when we go wrong. But not too powerful an opposition that can frustrate everything that you want to do, you see?"

I think but don't repeat aloud of course: *not too powerful an opposition...*

My sense is he is going a little too fast here, so I try to pull him back a little: "But UMNO [United Malays National Organization] has been the dominant party forever, just like Japan's LDP [Liberal Democratic Party] had been so dominant for a long time ... and of course you had that brush-up with your former deputy PM, Anwar Ibrahim, which in the West looked like you don't much like serious opposition either."

To make a long story short, Anwar was first indicted in 1998 when Dr Mahathir was still PM—indicted on sodomy charges, jailed and eventually freed. Ten years later, with a different government in power, Anwar was charged again more or less for the same violation.

Dr M grimaces: "Yeah, I know. They say that I don't tolerate opposition."

I also mention that even though Dr M is out of power, the former PM also did just about everything he could to pull the rug from under his successor, Abdullah Badawi. Let's ease into this point this way.

"Well, you're a hard act to follow. I mean, you have a dynamic personality and I don't think you burdened your people with too many dull moments. To your fans you were like the magician of Malaysia. So you'd be hard to follow. You know, LKY was hard to follow, but they let his son cool his heels for a while and brought in Goh Chok Tong as the interim. But the interim lasted 14 years. I guess most people thought Goh did a very good job. In fact, some people liked him better than Lee."

"I know, but the old guy's still in the saddle you know?"

"What?"

"LKY is still there. He never lets go. I let go. He is keeping a lid on the [*indistinct*]—"

"The what?"

"The purse strings. He controls them."

That, if true, strikes me as a bit of news. There's no ready way to prove or disprove it, of course. Undoubtedly he's referring to Singapore's sovereign wealth fund, which is immense, rather than the regular annual governmental budget. But it does seem like something a fox like Mahathir might know about.

We move on: "Yeah, it's interesting. LKY once said in an interview for my newspaper column that he feared, after he left, that somehow the 'ultras' [radical Muslims] would get control of the government in Malaysia, and that Malaysia would invade Singapore. Any chance of that?"

He gazes at me as if I am a lunatic: "No chance, no chance at all. Well, uh, we let them [Singapore] go. They were with us, before; they were part of Malaysia. But we let them go, and they became a great metropolis and have done very well for themselves.

We're not angry with them because of that. Of course, they must treat us properly. Simple things like we want to build a bridge to replace the causeway, but they object. I mean, not that they object, but they refuse to build on their half unless of course we give them certain kinds of concessions, like selling them sand for their reclamation. Selling sand for reclamation is like selling part of your country to other people."

"I see."

I really don't. The sand issue seems petty to me, but I am not prepared to spend a lot of space in this book on sand. (My view: if you have extra sand, then sell it, and make some money; and if you don't have any extra, don't. It's not exactly an issue of national security. Oh well … the shifting sands of petty peninsular diplomacy.)

Dr M continuing: "You know, his fear is completely unfounded. Malaysians have never had any aggressive intentions. You know, south Thailand actually was a part of Malaysia, but we have never tried to, well, invade a country, or do anything with that."

"Right, you never have. In fact, the only time you had a serious problem was with Sukarno in Indonesia."

"Yeah, and that is because they attacked us. We had to defend ourselves."

"Yeah, and I like your view that you don't need an arms race with Singapore."

"Right, what for?"

"Who needs it?"

He says: "Because they are sending some F-16s for an exhibition. Of course, they want to show they have F-16s, because if people want to exhibit the F-16, it must be the Americans that are building and selling these things, not Singapore. But if Singapore wants to show them off, that's fine. We're not afraid of their F-16s, you see, because in the end, when you fight the war, you have to come down to the ground. And you come down to the ground and fight with handguns. See, that is more important than all the bombs from up in the air."

"If you want to take over territory."

"Yeah."

It is time to ask the Big One: "So tell me, what is your true view of Lee Kuan Yew?"

Dr Mahathir swivels, looks skeptically at me, as if maybe I really don't want to know what he thinks: "He's not satisfied with what he has. He's a big frog in a small pond. He's had ambitions to become prime minister of Malaysia. And of course the Tunku, the first prime minister, was not keen on that. So in the end of course Tunku realized he had to move Kuan Yew out. When he was a member of parliament, Malaysian parliament, I had a lot of debate with him. He tends to lecture people. The people in Parliament dislike that. So, I made it uncomfortable for him, so he didn't like me."

He takes a deep breath, swivels to look out the window, and sighs: "So, once I went to Singapore on an official visit, as another ASEAN country. The first thing that happened to me, which annoyed me, was that I was not treated as the leader of a country. Normally, when somebody, a prime minister, visits another prime minister, you go down and receive him—"

"Red carpet."

"Not just red carpet, you go down yourself!"

"Who'd they send?"

"They sent me a protocol officer, and then I was put in a room, a holding room waiting for the big man, and then Lee saw me … so, afterward I replied in kind. I call this the Singapore Protocol."

I'm not sure exactly what he means, but somehow it sounds funny and I laugh.

"So, when his minister or prime minister comes here, that's how I do it."

I now get the message: UNCIVIL reciprocation. "Is that the term now used in the Malaysian government—someone you don't like, and so then you give them the Singapore Protocol?"

"I don't know about the present, if that happens. But when he came here recently, he didn't come to see me."

Dr M says nothing for what seems like a long time. Then he says, sighing: "People look at him as an intellectual, as something more than just an ordinary politician, so he's always invited to give his views on things, and to that extent he is something bigger than Singapore. The fact remains that he is the mayor of Singapore. This is something that he doesn't like. He wants to be big, you see, and he feels that we took away his opportunity to lead a real country."

"You took away … what was the word you said?"

"Opportunity." That is, to lead Malaysia, when Singapore was asked to leave in 1965.

"Mhm, right."

"But I think he will go down in history as a very remarkable intellectual and a politician at the same time, which is not a very often thing. But the fact is that he just cannot move out of this ... it is there."

I lighten the mood, and half-jokingly thank Dr Mahathir for providing us Western journalists with such good copy over the years in his many delightfully sizzling public jousts with Lee.

"It was always very entertaining, you know."

Then Dr M surprises me: "Actually we really did it all for you journalists!"

It's not hard to laugh at that, and I do.

"Well, we appreciated it," I said. "We appreciate the drama."

In all the conversations with Lee Kuan Yew for Book One of the "Giants of Asia" series, I was never once in doubt about whether he was kidding or serious. (He was always totally serious.) But with Dr M, you cannot always be sure … at first, anyway.

A Mahathir Political Point

**Do unto others rhetorically, as in fact
they do unto you, if they do it in public
… or in a way that can become known
to the public, or you will lose face.**

From Asia With Love

The values debate ... too much freedom?
... America's closet elitists ... too much criticism?

OF what real value are so-called Asian values?

The main point of them, it would appear, is that they are unlike American values. Or, further, unlike broad European values.

East Asian Confucian values arising from a Chinese culture are arguably coherent. They emphasize loyalties to parents, community, village and state that are deeply rooted in the cultural history. Islamic values might not have the same exact definition, except for their emphasis on a reverence for the leader.

But, however deep or shallow their sincerity, are they really all that good a thing for the societies that are (or are claimed to be) so deeply grounded in them, whether Asian, Islamic or ... Islama-Asian?

Maybe—just maybe—they are of more value to those who govern than to the governed?

This is the cynical view. After all, stripped of all possible sophistication and complexity, you can almost summarize Asian values in one short three-word sentence: Daddy knows best. (Or substitute for Daddy, if you want, the Government, the Establishment, the Community, the Family.)

We are so often exposed to the oft-heard pitch about the transcendent wonder of Asian values that we should imagine that governing an Asian country might not, after all, be such an impossibly tough grind.

Just consider this: that every single proclaimed Asian value, by the very definition of the Asian-value evangelists, would appear to be close buddies of such proclaimed civic virtues as community allegiance, group and national loyalty and almost unthinking respect for hierarchy. This is to say nothing of semi-religious obeisance to the maximum leader (a version of so-called filial piety).

What Western leader wouldn't want to practice politics in a polity suffused with such norms? Especially when you consider the brutal contrast of 'Western values'. Here, back West, we take pride in the relentless prioritization of individualism (to the point of righteous disobedience), of self-interest (to the point of ethical blindness and arrant selfishness) and of constant criticism of leaders (to the point of self-destructive negativism).

So if you're a bossy type, what's not to like with those values Asian?

No one has held forth more often on the Asian values perspective than Dr M (and Singapore's Lee Kuan Yew). They have been practically Asian values evangelists supreme.

So on this sensitive but vital topic I try to draw Dr M out a little, hoping he might expose the whole thing as one big fraud that smart Asians use to pull the wool over the eyes of gullible Westerners (like me).

So I slip this across his desk: "The business—the so-called 'Asian values' stuff—that you and your Singapore counterpart have talked so much about over the decades. Isn't that a lot of baloney? Asian values, please! I mean, isn't that just a cover so you authoritarians can do whatever you want, or is there actually something to it?"

Dr M laughs at the sarcastic parry. You have to admire the way he reacts to most things. It's really hard to get him visibly upset ... unless he wants deliberately to show temper.

"Well, Tom, I think there is something to it. I mean, you cannot say that everyone has the same set of values. We are different. It is because we have different sets of values that our achievements are so different."

"But you really don't believe in democracy, do you?"

"Well, we have a democracy in the sense that you can remove a leader without having to have a revolution. So, you can vote him out. That's democracy to me. Other elements are appendices added on to a democracy, but the essence of democracy is the right to choose or to bring down the leader. That's what we have. But, of course, for the West, they say no! Oh, you have to have liberal democracy—freedoms of these, and freedoms of those, and all that."

But what's wrong with that?

Dr Mahathir would suggest that the loudest advocates of democracy are closet elitists, rather than sincere passionate democrats: "In all this you have found one thing: that our newspapers do not criticize the government enough, or they hold back and do not criticize at all. But that's not really the fault of the leader. The natural tendency of people in this country—that's where our values differ from the West—is not to be critical of the leader. You must give the leader support, and the Western press can never understand this. And they say, 'Oh, you are controlling the people.' We're not controlling the people. These people impose upon themselves censorship."

It's hard to imagine more than one average person at a Los Angeles Starbucks agreeing with that, and I don't buy it much myself (though I buy a little more of it than many Western journalists), so I return to the values question.

"Those values, are those values deep in your culture, do you think? Or … what drives them?"

Mahathir thinks for a few minutes. You can almost hear him. The air-conditioning in the Petronas Tower One is almost completely silent. The window over his shoulder is aflame with sunlight, but inside it is cool and pastel. The only tension in this large room is Dr M's thoughts competing like late trains for the last disembarkation spot at the station.

Then he offers what in effect is a moral argument: "I think it's wrong that you are *against* simply because you must be *against*. I mean you have to have a reason to be *against*. If you have no reason, and simply because this is the tradition—this is what we [in the media] think you should do, and so you [the leader] do it—I think that is wrong, and I think a leader needs to be supported. If you undermine the leader the moment he's elected, and start this game of undermining him, and making life difficult for him, and making it impossible for him to carry out a program which you want him to carry out, which was why you elected him in the first place…"

He has a bit of a point. It's a point that can be pushed into terrible dictatorship, to be sure, but it doesn't have to be.

So I chip in with a few points: "And also, too, what the journalists, particularly in the West, assume when they're interviewing somebody is they think that the leader necessarily must be incompetent—and that they can do the job better than him or her. But have you ever met a journalist who interviewed you who you thought could be a better PM than you were?"

"No."

"No, right? Because it takes a lot, right?"

Dr M makes a face like he swallowed a live eel: "Yeah. If you have no responsibility, it's much easier to say that we should be doing these things or those things, but there are constraints to everything that you want to do. You have to take into consideration all kinds of factors. It is not just, 'Well, this is good, I must do it.' You have to say, 'If I do it, what would my supporters say?' for example. I have to think about the environment in which I function."

That seemed like an odd formulation for such a famous soft-authoritarian strongman: "Well, Dr Mahathir, a famous Machiavelli dictum is that it's better for the Leader to be both feared and loved, but if only one is possible it is better for him to be feared. How about you?"

"No, I want to be loved."

"By as many people as possible?"

He swirls clockwise in his chair, looks out the window at the vast cityscape in front of him, pauses, then says: "Yes, by as many people as possible. One reason why I let go in 2003 … I stepped down at a time when I was very popular, even now I am popular. I go around and people come up to me, shake my hand, take my picture and even say thank you. You see, I don't want to step down maybe after achieving certain things, and then step down with people hating me. That, I don't like. I did what I could to make people not hate me. But, of course some people will hate you, whatever you do. That is acceptable to me."

One Mahathir expert has written that the former PM always believed he was acting as an extension of Malaysian popular will. I say this to Dr M: "This expert said, 'Vox popular—Mahathir equals vox popular.' Did you always think that, if you felt something deep inside of you, and your intuition told you it was the right way to go, that you were always reflecting, somehow, the Malaysian national desire?"

That one seems to irritate him a little: "Not quite."

"No?"

"No, it's not true! I spent a lot of time criticizing my own people—the Malays. And I told them at the end, 'I spent 22 years telling you to do what is right, and you are still not doing it.' So, I don't do all the popular things. I do what I think is right, even though I might anticipate a lot of objection."

Mahathir has credibility here. Ever since the publication of his controversial book *The Malay Dilemma* in 1970, modern Malaysia's most famous leader has often laid it on the line with his Malays: you are a bunch of lazy *bumiputras* (this is the word used for Malaysian natives; literally, people of the soil), so wake up and start studying more, start working harder, start producing more.

The *bumiputra* problem has been a paradox. Help them with special government assistance (education quotes, job spots) and you do compensate for the allegedly innate laid-back attitude. But over time the culture of assistance makes the native Malays even less independent. Only if the affirmative-action-for-the-majority program is designed to be short term—that is, transitional—can it be sure of avoiding a permanent culture of welfare for the majority. In recent comments to associates and occasional blog comments and articles, the former PM has hinted at the downside of the policy that he so vigorously advanced when in office.

Pushing it along: "But you take the view then that once you decide that something is the right way to go, and you figure out, in the environment that you have, that there will be resistance, but it's doable to get there, and you think it's important for Malaysia, you know, it's going to be painful to get there, though it won't blow the place up, so you're going to do it?"

He nods: "Yes. But I think it's difficult, because this is a multiracial country. We have so many different opinions and we have to cope with them. That we manage at all is, to me, an achievement."

Democratic theory seemingly should embrace a multiethnic society, but in Asia, as elsewhere, the reality grinds against theory with all the menace of edgy teutonic plates. Rightly or wrongly, ethnic tension seems never too far below the surface of Southeast Asia.

Asian soft-authoritarians (not to mention the harder ones like those in Beijing) hate the inherent risks associated with so-called total freedom of expression. They also find nervous-making the pat philosophical assumption of one person, one vote. They put it this way, as I formulate it for Dr M:

"It could be said that one person, one vote means that the homeless person in the street, in the gutter, who's drunk or stoned, who's basically thrown his life away—that person's vote is worth the same as the emergency-room doctor's. Does that make sense to you? I mean, I asked this last year of Singapore Minister Mentor Lee Kuan Yew, and he said, in effect, 'It makes no sense whatsoever to me.' So I said, 'You're not exactly a real big fan of one man, one vote, are you?' and he said, 'No.' "

Dr M always chuckles when exposed to views seemingly even more conservative than his own: "Democracy is a good system, but it has its weaknesses. You must understand the workings of democracy to make it work. You know, there are limitations, and some people seem to think that if you go to war and make such-and-such country a democratic country [U.S. in Iraq], you'll solve all their problems. It's the wrong thing to do. People must understand democracy before they accept democracy, because there is a limit to freedom. There is no absolute freedom for anyone."

Please note that Mahathir's anti-Americanism as well as his blind allegiance to pan-Islamic policy can easily be over-estimated. In 1990, for example, he instructed his UN ambassador to vote in favor of the use of force to eject the Iraqi army from Kuwait, angering many Muslim leaders and their followers.

At home, however, he always seeks to emphasize a stark cleavage between Malaysia's Asian values and America's Western values.

Me saying: "Right, you think that the Western definition of freedom is sometimes defined in so broad a way that it's almost a prescription for irresponsibility?"

No hesitation here: "It is. But when you imagine the concept, maybe for the first time, you might think in terms of a certain circumscribed thing within some limit, and so this is fine. But the moment you say freedom is something that we must uphold at all costs, then the high cost comes in! People will make use of freedom to do all kinds of wrong things."

"For example…"

"I mean, you say, 'I will defend you; your freedom of speech I must defend in every way.' But if somebody comes up to a person and curses him and the man gets angry and it goes to the court, and the court says, 'Sorry, that's his freedom, that's his right.' "

From this perspective, he might have been wondering about essential American sanity over a 2010 appeals court decision upholding the right of anti-gay church protestors to picket the funeral of a young Marine killed in Iraq. The Marine happened to be gay. The church extremists made their presence noisily known at the funeral. An appeals court upheld their right. The father of the Marine took the appeal's decision to the Supreme Court.

Dr M and his Muslim faith have no formal tolerance for homosexuality, but in his mind public law and order come first. So he shakes his head as if unbelieving that such courts and legal reasoning exist anywhere on a sane planet. But like any good American, I was brought up to believe in the relative inviolability of the Bill of Rights.

Even so, one would have to agree that freedom from restraint is not necessarily freedom for irresponsibility. As an editor of an American newspaper, for example, I would be chary of permitting ridicule of almost any religion.

Continuing: "Remember the cartoons, the anti-Allah cartoons in the Danish newspaper some years ago? Theoretically you should have the right to say whatever you want, but if you know it's going to infuriate millions and millions and millions of people, what's the point? Shouldn't you have some self-restraint? And then people say, well but that's censorship. No, censorship is when the government says you can't do X, but self-restraint can be a good thing, right?"

"Yeah."

That was such an easy sell. I'm talking too much.

A Mahathir Political Point

Think first of the rights and security of the group before the rights of the individual.

Moonraker

**The Proton project … motivating the Malays
… shoot for the moon? … a PM's pay!**

BIG egos launch big projects—but sometimes they crash on their launching pads.

Near the start of his presidency, John F. Kennedy declared it a U.S. national goal to put a man on the moon. A man eventually set foot there, but, before and after, there were misfires and tragedies. But in retrospect, most observers would assess that enormous national effort as worthwhile.

Near the start of his prime ministership, Mahathir Mohamad launched a national car program known as Proton. At first everyone scoffed at the presumption; and even today many Malaysians doubt its utility—or even think of it as a kind of movable (if at least horizontal) Petronas-Tower-type ego-trip.

Like the U.S. space program, the Proton car project required the continual push from both shoulders of the nation's leader to survive. In the end, shortly after Mahathir left office, the Proton project went into decline. In the final analysis it probably lost more money than it made. But economically speaking, the country did perhaps benefit somewhat from the forced need to develop an automotive sector, both in technology and in manpower training.

Mahathir simply could not imagine Malaysia moving forward without major industrialization. In fact, in both the U.S. and Malaysian cases, these showcase projects got off the ground through the solid fuel of the egos of the national leaders. JFK never lived to see Americans landing on the moon, of course. But Mahathir believes, even today, that Malaysia would not have moved into higher economic orbit without the Proton car project.

It all makes you wonder what it takes to be a national leader. The successful ones tend to be more similar than dissimilar, notwithstanding huge national and cultural differences.

So I ask: "In order to be an effective prime minister, is there an ideal education for the prime minister of Malaysia or is it a combination of personal characteristics? I mean, you went to medical school … could you imagine creating a public policy school that would be training leaders of Malaysia for the future? Or is it that you can't do it that programmatically?"

Mahathir shrugs and throws up his hands: "Yeah, you can train people who may become leaders, but there is no formula, really. You have to also depend upon the character of the person. You see, character plays a really important role in a leader. You can't say, 'You can do A, B, C and D and therefore you can become a leader.' That's nothing, no. The ability to weigh things, to actually think what the other people are going to say to what you are doing—you have to have that…"

"Intuition."

"Right."

"So how do you define political intuition or leadership? What is the Mahathir definition?"

He tugs a little on his jacket, stares down, then at me: "Well, you must be able to gauge or to decide whether things should be done or not, even though it may make you a little bit unpopular or even quite unpopular. For example, when I became prime minister, way back in 1981, I decided that we should build a Malaysian national car, and I met a lot of opposition on that issue, including from my own deputy. He said that it could not be done … how can a developing country build its own car? But I thought it could be done. I was willing to take the risk. And I felt that I could make it a success and therefore later on, the people would see that what we did was something they should support. And, in the end they supported the idea."

I just knew he would raise this example: "Well, one of your reasons, as I understand it, that you wanted to do the Proton was that it wasn't just a line of cars, it was a whole industrial sector that you wanted in this country, right?"

He nods.

This I have to add, undiplomatically: "Now, I have to say, I notice that when *Car and Driver* magazine did its annual ten-best cars, Proton never got on the list. So, how can you say that that was a success?"

He looks at me but I hold his gaze. We're not going to agree on everything. It would bother me a lot if we did.

A few seconds pass—maybe he is a bit annoyed now, but no one blinks.

Him finally saying: "In the context of Malaysia? Yes, it is a success. If you compare Malaysia—not with the United States or with Japan—but with other developing countries, there are no other developing countries that have been able to produce their own national car, and the spin-off is that we stimulate the engineering industry in this country. So, that was one of the objectives."

Malaysia's Proton car program was a huge stretch for his country. Was it a fool's errand? The best overall readable evaluation of the economics of the effort can be found in Barry Wain's meticulously detailed 2009 book *Malaysian Maverick*. What's perhaps most surprising, though, is not that the Proton project came to look like the proverbial dog with three legs but that the car industry came to be born at all.

If nothing else, the Proton was further evidence (as if any were needed) of Dr M's protean will. So I try to tease him a little.

I say: "If a national car program would stimulate national pride, then why not go for broke and start with the space program and shoot for the moon?"

He ignores the arrant insolence and doesn't laugh at all. He won't go for the bait. "No," he says flatly.

(In fact, just before he stepped down, he established the outlines of a Malaysian space program.)

I try not to lose a beat: "But … it is in fact your honest view of the Proton program that, even though it didn't produce the world's greatest car, it was, nonetheless, in the context of Malaysia anyhow, a positive success."

"It was. It gave pride to the people. But it took time of course, before it got to that stage. You have to *make* it a success."

"And you would do it again?"

"I would."

Every new country sets out at a different starting point. Left to fend for itself as a new nation in 1957 (the Japanese having been decimated and the British having basically shrunk), Malaysia had to overcome numerous daunting obstacles.

One of them was the fast-growing realization that the Malays as a people would never challenge the Chinese in the workaholism category. In fact, once in power, Dr M and his administration generated government policies that gave the native Malays all kinds of economic and opportunity preferences over the Chinese and Indians.

Let us pause for a positive word about the Malay culture, however. There is something healthy about a people who are loath to work themselves to death. Is there not something that needs to be said for a people who, generally speaking, find more to life than work? As a career workaholic myself, I would like to stop this book mid-stream and offer a standing ovation (and then slink away on holiday … but I cannot!).

What's more, qualities of kindness and self-deprecation are values that are not exactly criminal. These days, those values may be more characteristic of the calm Malaysian countryside than teeming Kuala Lumpur, but they are embedded in the culture, and simply tearing down that culture will not help us understand it.

Alas, not enough of the rest of the world is so laid-back that Malay mellowness works as a feasible formula for regional and international economic competitiveness. The suspicion grew that the average Malay, as if in a caricature of the average Argentinean (all play, no work), was more cut out for the relatively sane enjoyment of life than full-speed-ahead economic achievement.

But was this analysis correct and fair? One thing is for sure: it has been the good doctor's unwavering diagnosis of the Malay character that his fellow Malay would be the person always cuddled under the shade of a tree half asleep—and into whose ears shouting was the only effective modality of communication. By contrast, the minority Chinese residents of the country were generally viewed as steroid-fueled self-starters, and the Indians were appreciated for having their own ancient but effective ways.

Dr M explains what he means by reference to another Asian culture that in many respects he deeply admires. He sweeps his right hand forward from the center of his chest up into the air as if flinging something skyward: "For example, if you take the Japanese … their sense of shame is very, very strong, to the point where if you feel you have done something that is shameful, you commit hara-kiri. Do you find any Europeans doing that? Or Americans?"

Sorry for intruding on this serious conversation with a joke—but I have to say this to him: "No, we just get expensive lawyers."

He almost falls on the desk laughing.

Dr M continuing: "You know, the Japanese want to produce the most perfect things. I mean, if you look at their wickerwork, their bamboo products, it is so fine because they have that in them."

Insider Asian cultural note: many Asian leaders can hardly believe the dimensions and duration of the Japanese economic downturn. For the longest time, quite a few non-Japanese Asian leaders had been great admirers of workaholic Japan, though mostly in private, while of course bashing them at every other war-crimes opportunity before their publics.

They still tend to admire the national qualities of patriotism, discipline, work ethic, competent management and intimate cooperation between the private sector and the government. Mahathir believes that to some extent Malaysia's economic progress in the 80s and 90s derived from its partial imitation of Japanese economic and business ways.

After taking office, the turn toward Japan was one of Dr M's first moves. It is absolutely hilarious that shortly after becoming PM, Mahathir put out two major new economic policies: the first, in anger with the British, was known as 'Buy British Last'. The intent was to flatten British sales in Malaysia and punch those arrogant ex-colonialists in the face. The second, in emulation of Japanese economic practices (and to some extent South Korean), was called the 'Look East Policy'.

He is right. It's not hard to be an admirer of Japanese perfectionism.

Me saying: "It is amazing, isn't it? You know, when they put their mind to something, and they say, 'Okay, we're going to be *ichiban* in this, we're going to be the best in this.' They are unbelievable."

He nods: "It's their values. The Japanese worker comes to work earlier than the time required. His group will then discuss what is the target for today, then set out to achieve that target. You don't see that happening in the U.S."

"Do you see it in Malaysia?"

"Only in Proton, because we sent some of our workers to Japan to teach them Japanese work ethics."

Proton, according to Mahathir's many critics, was the world's biggest automotive white elephant since … well … in fact, since the late 50s, when Ford came out with the Edsel, its worst selling car ever in the U.S.

But for Dr M, as we observe, the Proton was far more than a mere car product; it was a calculated gamble to implant a patch of Japanese workplace efficiency via a national program. It worked even if it didn't work.

Me continuing: "You have been evangelical on the issue of the work ethic, but the problem for you is that your Malays, a little bit like the Thais or say the Argentineans, are generally exceptionally pleasant to be around but are not the world's leading go-getters. You feel they're certainly not working all the time, like the Koreans who do indeed seem to be working all the time! You saw your prime ministership as a way to redress the imbalance. You wanted to emphasize the work part, and you figured your people would know how to do the fun part without your guidance!"

He throws his head up in laughter.

"But on the work part, you look at the Japanese because it seems to be very embedded in them."

Malaysia's long college-football-style rivalry with neighboring Singapore, which is mainly Chinese, would have made a Chinese-style model of emulation politically impossible for Mahathir, until relatively further into his career, when at one point it seemed as if he could do almost anything he wanted.

He nods.

I ask, only because I am curious, as China rises in Asia and is starting to eclipse Japan economically: "Do you take the view that the Japanese are far from finished yet, on the world stage?"

"They are far from finished. They have tremendous capabilities, and it is their value system."

"Still to be near the top somewhere?"

"I mean from producing some of the worst products, before—"

"Right."

"…they have graduated to become the finest, I mean the most meticulous workers, producing the best products in the world."

That's what top Asian leaders truly think of Japan, no matter what complaining and bashing they do in public to observe (or politically exploit) the horrible memory of the Japanese colonial and wartime occupations.

Mahathir believes many Malaysians now understand his approach to energizing the culture. He proudly recounts a recent holiday reception at his home the other day that attracted thousands. They just streamed in, he claims, to say hi! to Mr and Mrs former PM.

"Thousands," he says. "A few aides hung around but no security police. Can you imagine that kind of casual, open scene in the U.S.?"

Mahathir is still in the news every third day, it seems, and his supporters insist Malaysia seems not quite as together now as during those 22 years.

Even so, a powerful man essentially out of power is one of the saddest sights in politics. Perhaps Dr M intrudes himself into the everyday debate because Malaysia itself doesn't quite know how to accommodate the energies and experience of its former leaders. After all, it has only been an independent nation since 1957.

I try this on him: "We have a tradition in America, and I think it's one of our best traditions. We fully employ our ex-presidents. They do pretty well. I mean, Carter was a weak president but is a very good ex-president. I think Clinton is doing good work. I don't know about George W. Bush. To be charitable, I guess he hasn't been an 'ex' long enough to make his mark. But are the former prime ministers of Malaysia properly used?"

His usual spitfire response is delayed. He considers for a few ticks of the clock, then says: "Not quite, but on the other hand, you can make yourself useful without the government being involved. You don't have to advise the government or anything like that, but there are lots of things to do as an individual, and the government gives me amenities, which makes life easy for me."

On his desk is a bound copy of his typed memoirs. He is making changes galore in them, doesn't seem happy about them—he admits that they are taking forever mainly because he keeps changing them. And because the Malaysian government is throwing the iron censorship curtain up on pages it believes affect national security. Dr M is not amused.

I wonder whether he'd make as much money from them as the usual memoirs of an American president. The publisher's advance on Clinton's memoirs was well more than US$10 million.

He shakes his head at that: "See, I'm paid a pension of my last drawn paid (paycheck), which is 10,000 Malaysian ringgit, and that is about 3,000 USD … less than 3,000 USD."

"Three thousand dollars weekly?"

That would then be about right. It would compute to about $150,000 a year. Even that is not so much for a former political giant of Asia—but it's ok.

"No," he laughs. "*Monthly.*"

This is hard for me to believe: "Three thousand a month, U.S.? Gosh, that's like a meager U.S. journalists' pension. Comes to $36,000 a year!"

"Yeah."

I almost stare at him. "That's … not a lot."

He tries not to look uncomfortable. "I don't know, but I don't need money because they provide me with a car. Oil and electricity is paid for."

"Because you're a former PM."

"Former PM, yeah … so …"

"That's the way it should be." But still, he must have saved part of his salary during those 22 years or … whatever.

"Yeah, yeah, well … even as a PM I never bothered about how much money I made. When I first became PM they paid me 8,000 Malaysian ringgit, which is about 2,100 USD."

He means … *a month*. This whole compensation discussion doesn't compute for me. This is what they think of their prime ministers in Malaysia—to pay them so little?

On the other hand, Asia is one place where strong-armed leaders, and/or their relatives, have been known to compensate themselves off-the-book. For decades in Indonesia, the family of President Suharto lived legendarily well. By contrast, in Singapore, "no one"—as I say to Mahathir—"has ever said that LKY has a secret Swiss bank account; he may, but no one has ever said it, much less proved it." In the grand sliding scale of official corruption, then, where is Malaysia on the Asian map? Somewhere between Indonesia and Singapore?

I ask him: "Is it as simple as the fact, that in addition to your having been an actually competent leader, as he was, that you're not greedy?"

Because if he is, I think to myself, someone is paying him. And it's not the average Malaysian taxpayer.

He answers firmly: "No, I said to you the real reward is achievement."

"You're not greedy?"

Dr M comes from a common rural family, one of nine children; wealth is not part of his inheritance. "Being greedy? You know when I was a student I had only 20 cents in my pocket and wanted to buy a plate of noodles. I went to the hawker and asked, 'Can I have 20 cents worth of noodles?' and he says, 'No, 50 cents. It must be 50 cents for a plate, or nothing at all.' "

We laugh. Like most adults who grew up poor, such slights forever remain permanent cavernous indents in their minds.

"So now I tell myself how many plates of noodles can I eat? I mean, with the pay that I get, I have enough to eat; I have enough for all I need. So, what was the need for having more?"

I nod. "As I used to say to my students at UCLA when I was teaching there, how many BMWs do you need to be happy?"

"Yeah." He actually seemed to like that.

"And then you go back to that famous line by Gandhi: 'There is enough for our needs but not enough for our greeds.' "

Then me adding: "But there is another historically great line about wealth. It's Chinese, from none other than Mao's successor Deng Xiaoping: 'To be rich is glorious.' "

He says nothing to that.

I ask: "I know no one in office 22 years can be a model of policy consistency, but you have said somewhere that the best thing that the rich can do for the poor is to stay rich, right?"

"Yeah, that's about other people, not about me!"

We both laugh.

Still, he can't be really pressed for money if all these years after leaving office, his memoirs—the usual source of an ex-leader's quick and honest reward for hard service—still aren't done!

I end the discussion by mentioning the various probes said to be underway in Malaysia, involving alleged misuse or misappropriation of government money.[2] Allegations include rake-offs from all manner of public projects. Outsiders have claimed that some of Dr M's relatives are worth plenty, and that the good doctor himself has funds and shares stashed here and there (and especially in Japan) and everywhere.

Nothing has ever been proven. And perhaps never will, at least in the short run. Whatever the validity of the rumors (and that is all they are), the bottom line is that the dominant party, UMNO, controls the bureaucracy that runs the police. There's no chance of the police getting out of hand and arresting the country's most famous living political figure, right?

"Well, you're not in jail," I say.

"Not quite," he responds slowly.

As I have said, sometimes you just don't know when he is serious or when he is joking.

---

2 For the best discussion of this, again, see veteran journalist Barry Wain's comprehensive book, *Malaysian Maverick* (2009).

The Men With the Golden Guns

**Trusting the cops ... no palace guards here
... the limits of political loyalty ... betrayal**

STRONGMEN fear not the ostentatious flex of the strong arm.

And so our own good doctor is an almost unapologetic advocate of using police power to ensure domestic tranquility (and his party's political hegemony) if and when things threaten to get out of hand.

But the gap between the politically sophisticated Mahathir and any number of vulgar standard-brand dictators exceeds the width—and indeed—depth of the Grand Canyon. He accepts that any recourse to overt repression is an inglorious moment for a ruler—a tacit admission of the failure of suave and persuasive political management.

It seems like our 'soft' authoritarian has a 'soft' spot in his heart for more nuanced measures of social and political control.

He also accepts that exercising the option of a police-ordered operation even for genuine national-security reasons can be misinterpreted (or, in the less than genuine cases of national-security, quite correctly understood) as the autocrat's blanket repression of dissent and opposition.

He also accepts that police intervention in the political arena can go badly wrong. That, more or less, is what happened in Malaysia in 1987 when Dr M, then-prime minister—but a-half dozen years in power—ordered his most infamous crackdown.

We talk about this inglorious episode in his second floor office in suburban Putrajaya (it is only 84 stories lower than his other one in Kuala Lumpur!), the clean if somewhat arid administrative capital of the country. It too was erected within Dr M's reign, along with a sweeping plan to hi-tech the country via a development scheme called the Multimedia Super Corridor. This latter was designed to be a kind of grandiose Malaysian Silicon Valley. It got off the ground in the late 90s but never quite took off.

Putrajaya, named after the independent country's first PM, Tunku Abdul Rahman Putra, lies south of the historic capital, KL, and closer to the big international airport, though somewhere in the middle of a suburban nowhere.

So here we are…

He is sitting behind his desk quietly. He doesn't look like a cop, though he probably might have made a good one. And his international reputation as a hard-boiled (if 'soft') authoritarian inevitably makes you wonder about his feelings about the use of police and security force to achieve social and political control.

I start by noting jokingly that while Dr M himself has never been arrested, he has ordered the arrest of many others. In the world outside Malaysia, he is regarded, rightly or wrongly, as someone who is not afraid to throw down the rug of social repression.

Perhaps the most notorious example occurred in 1987.

I say: "Alright. Going back to Operation Lalang; L-A-L-A-N-G, how do you pronounce it?" (*Lalang* is Malay for weedy grass that is plucked and thrown away—get it?)

"La-lang."

I am referring to the well-known (well-known around the Malay Peninsula, anyway) ordeal of October 1987. With serious ethnic tensions (allegedly) in the air, police arrested opposition leaders and social activists, and in effect closed down newspapers. The reason given was imminent domestic unrest. The country was flabbergasted, stunned and resentful.

I try to ease into a touchy issue: "Looking back … really necessary? Any regrets about that? How do you … how do you look at that, historically?"

"Perhaps we, on hindsight—"

"Which is always 20/20."

Dr M rocks a little in his chair and peers around the room as if to see that the coast is clear. Then he starts pointing his right index finger into the air: "Yeah. *Regrets* … I mean you have to trust the police, because you have to work with them. They are the people who have to look after security, and when they advise you that the tension is very high, that it might explode into racial riots, and they need to take this action, you can't tell them no. You don't, you see, because you know less than they do. See, and you have to trust the people who are the implementers. I have no means of verifying everything that they say."

Perhaps not, but calling in the police to handle what might be a political issue may be an assignment of delicacy well above their pay grade.

So me pushing: "Right, but the police mentality is a bit like the crude military mentality, where force is the first option. Now, you're a soft authoritarian, not a hard authoritarian, and you as a doctor look—it seems to me—at issues of social control with more nuance and sophistication. So, just to go back to that one more time, would there have been a better way of handling it?"

Dr M is clearly uncomfortable, but I sense he does not want to duck the question: "Well, I would have handled it differently, except that the police wanted to do these things because they say it is necessary..."

"To throw them in jail."

Sighing, he continues: "I actually met all of the opposition members [beforehand] and assured them that they would not be arrested. And you know what the police did? They arrested them. My credibility is gone."

"You must have been furious!"

It is doubtful that Mahathir easily accepts being made to look like a powerless leader, much less a fool. At least I assume he must have been furious and embarrassed.

"Yeah, but what can I do? You see, I have to accept that they are the people on the ground that makes a decision. I give very general authority to them."

He is speaking with a weary tone of inevitability.

Me continuing: "So your control even as prime minister over the police is not absolute?"

"No, not absolute. You have to learn to live with the people with the guns."

"That's a striking line. *You have to learn to live with the people with the guns.*"

Dr M shrugs his shoulders and raises his hands palms up to the ceiling: "Yeah, you don't have guns here [in the PM's office]. You don't have palace guards, you know, in Malaysia. Other people in other countries may have palace guards and they [the leadership] own a battalion or whatever. I don't have that. I depend upon the police for my own protection, and I have to trust them."

Pausing anew, Mahathir takes a deep breath: "You see, if they make a mistake, I take the blame. If they decide to detain people and people say it's wrong, well they did it under my time, so I must be responsible."

Leaders of his stature rarely speak this frankly about the double-edged police sword. He is either being clever in that he wants to lay the Lalang cock-up on the cops, or he wants to leave some basic truth with history, or perhaps both.

I say: "But then, does that make you to some extent a hostage of the people who have guns?"

He mulls that over: "To a certain extent ... everybody is. You see, you have to give people the means to enforce, and then of course they are better equipped than you are. You have to accept the fact that when they tell you that certain things need to be done, you have to respect them. If you keep running them down—there have been instances where they were run down by the government as being incompetent, corrupt and all that—and what happens then? Since we are corrupt [the police say to themselves], we will be corrupt, and since you say we are not good, we will not implement anything. So, if the police decide not to carry out their duty, what can you do? Okay, you set up a commission; what can a commission do?"

"Yeah, a few dumb newspaper stories."

"Yeah."

Me saying; "So you've got to work with the guns."

He seems a little down here: "Yeah, and if there is a problem with them, I talk with them. I talk privately with them and say, 'Look, this is wrong. You'd better do something about it.' But if you go and [publicly] run down the whole force, they will say, 'Well, why should I take all this [negativity and public criticism] from you? What can you do to me?' "

Me adding: "And of course, in any bureaucracy—in police, in health—there are going to be good people and bad people."

"That's right. I don't think all politicians are good, or all of them are bad. We always have a mixture, but the way you handle the people is very important. You must not undermine them completely or pull the carpet from under their feet—then, they become useless to you."

That has the ring of truth to it.

"After the 1987 incident, were you a little more reluctant to avail yourself of the police option?"

"No, but I thought I would be. See, I didn't like the ISA [the Internal Security Act], but I understand the necessity. But too frequent implementation and abuse of the power is bad."

That, of course, is precisely the criticism sometimes leveled at his governing style.

"Right. It needs to be used only in very special cases. Does the government of Malaysia have good control over ISA now?"

"Over?"

"Does the government of Malaysia have good control over ISA?"

"Yes."

"I mean compared say to Pakistan's control over its special branches." This is in reference to the Directorate of Inter-Services Intelligence (ISI) in Pakistan, which often appears to operate semi-independently of government oversight and control.

Dr M nods: "I mean if you look at other countries, they would abuse power like that … anytime, against opposition. But during my time when we had this Operation Lalang, I actually had our own party members arrested because the police recommended that they should be arrested and detained."

"Arrested because of subversive activity?"

"Because they were creating tension, racial tension."

Perhaps Dr M doesn't want to admit it, but that's a whole gray area of infractions which, interpreted too broadly, can land a person under ISA in jail for merely not agreeing with the government.

"Okay, but when during the Bush administration, when the aggressive interrogation and torture of prisoners in Iraq and Afghanistan, and of course from Guantanamo, became known ... were you surprised?"

Dr M's eyebrows shoot up: "Yes, I was surprised, because ... I was surprised that they should resort so quickly to detaining people without trial. They don't even have the law [that enables them to do that]. We have a law."

"You have the ISA."

"Yeah, you don't. And they [U.S. officials] don't and they were willing to break all—everything. I mean, torturing people is not acceptable and their strategy was approved by Congress, can you imagine that? I mean it's like me going to Parliament saying, 'You should allow me to torture people.' That's not acceptable, but in the U.S., they did that."

Not a few Westerners will laugh at the selective morality of that. When former deputy Anwar Ibrahim was grabbed by the police and arrested in 1998, he wound up sporting a black eye and stories about very rough treatment. His ordeal could be viewed as a kind of low-level torture. Mahathir's lectures on the moral obloquy of torture thus won't impress Anwar's supporters, or Western critics of Malaysia's human rights record, for their sincerity or instructional value. Even so, Mahathir's main point was that even the world's greatest democracy can find itself in areas of moral gray.

For now I move on: "I like your line, 'You know when you're dealing with the police they are a blunt instrument and you don't want to embarrass them publicly, you've got to make peace with the guns, you know?' Those little insights, those little touches … they teach people about what governance is really like. What it's really like is: you're not all-powerful, you've got to maneuver."

Mahathir nods. To me this was one of the more candid discussions by a former leader of a country about the paradox of selecting the option of police power to repress. It can blow up in your face—in anyone's face.

A Mahathir Political Point
Never embarrass the police publicly.
Make your points in private and hope
professional pride serves as the corrective.

ANWAR Ibrahim was Mahathir's number two for many years. The eloquent politician was widely believed to be next in line as PM. That never happened; he was arrested for sodomy and other charges in 1998.

It was widely thought that the police action had to have been authorized by Dr M himself. Ten years later, Anwar was arrested again on similar charges—but this time under a different prime minister when Mahathir was clearly out of power.

For Dr M, Anwar was a protégé who became an enemy. That blowup occurred in the run-up to the Asian Financial Crisis. Anwar was then deputy prime minister, personally ushered to that spot over the years by Dr M himself. The crisis triggered the fall of Suharto in Indonesia and added to the undoing of elected-President Kim Young Sam in South Korea. Perhaps Anwar figured the good Dr M's political head would be the next to roll downhill. To many observers, but especially Dr M himself, Anwar started to show his hand before Mahathir was ready to leave. Dr M believed Anwar was reaching out to the West for help to achieve that.

Anwar certainly endorsed the draconian economic reform conditions that Western aid agencies (especially the International Monetary Fund) were imposing on countries seeking IMF bailout aid. Anwar was all for that; Mahathir was all-out against it. Anwar surmised that Dr M's IMF opposition was more closely related to his desire to save his job than to protect his country. For his part, Mahathir believed that the fervency of Anwar's acceptance of and support for IMF was related less to economics than politics: the IMF's strict conditions for the loan money would make Mahathir unpopular and force him to resign. This would pave the way for Anwar's succession.

Dr M and his supporters viewed Anwar as too dangerously close to the West at a time when Dr M blamed the West and especially the U.S. for the worsening financial crisis. In truth, his former deputy had a number of supporters and admirers overseas, including in the Clinton administration and in the U.S. news media.

One was John Malott, the U.S. ambassador to Malaysia. A well-respected career American Foreign Service Officer, Malott saw Anwar as a comer whose views and values were closer to America's, and whose public rhetoric was less like screeching chalk on the blackboard. Anwar's political dossier included always saying the right things on human rights, keeping as tactfully quiet as possible on the Middle East question, and endorsing Washington's economic prescriptions for Malaysian reform.

But when Mahathir took Malaysia in an economic direction dramatically different—rejecting Western one-size-fits-all reform prescriptions—Anwar became the 'pro-Western agent within'. And so the strong-willed PM moved to have him removed.

Whether paranoia or proper Machiavellian insight, Mahathir today still insists that the sodomy charges were not trumped up, that homosexuality is seriously offensive to the normative culture of Malays, and that Anwar's secret relationship with powerful Western economic interests showed him to be more loyal to his ambitions than to his country.

Dr M attributes what happened with his long-time number two as a product of his deficiency in judging character.

Me easing into it: "My wife says to me that I have such a deep need to be liked by everyone that it makes me naïve in assessing people and not realizing that certain people not only don't like you, but will never like you and will wish you evil, and that no amount of your enormous charm is going to win them over. Do you have blind spots sometimes?"

"I got my blind spots, you know. You could say that I choose all of the wrong successors. The first deputy I chose decided to go against me, and then I had this man, Anwar. I thought I brought him up right up to the brink of it; he was going to succeed me.

Then I found that he was not suitable, and now of course he's going to town and running me down and things like that. People say, 'You don't know how to choose people, your successors.' Maybe it's because I was naïve."

It's hard to imagine the hard-nosed Dr M being naïve about anything, to tell the truth. But he does believe his nose for successors is seriously stopped up. In fact, when I asked him over and over again what he most regretted—his greatest failures—he invariably pointed to his ineptitude in his choice of top aides or successors.

He continues: "See, one of the things they like telling me is that I never change my staff. The people who are with me, like the man who brought you water just now, he's been with me 30 years. Of course, he's not perfect, he's got some weaknesses, but if I exchange him for another one I'm not going to get a perfect one either. So I try to stay with people and work out these things."

"Do you think of your staff as family?"

"Almost."

"You prize loyalty?"

"Yeah, and I am loyal to those colleagues and friends. I know that they have been accused of things, but until there is clear evidence that can stand up in a court of law, I had to give them the benefit of the doubt. But at the same time, of course if I think people just don't want a person, I have to respond, so I retire people. Not because I cannot get on, but because other people cannot."

"The person in question becomes radioactive."

"Yeah."

"So you prize loyalty, and you feel you reciprocate loyalty, and when someone makes a mistake, do you just write that off to we're human and imperfect and we're going to make mistakes?"

He shrugs: "Yeah, we are all imperfect. I make mistakes. So, I have to be tolerant of other people's mistakes, but you have to point out that there is a mistake and you need to correct it."

"And so if you indicate that you made a mistake, that's not a sign of weakness, actually, it's a sign of strength?"

"Yes."

"Right. Two or three mistakes that you've made that you wish you hadn't made ... can you think of a few?"

"One of my biggest mistakes was choosing my successor."

"Choosing your what?

"Successor."

"Oh."

A Mahathir Political Point

**The people you sometimes most have to trust
are the ones you most fear will turn on you.**

For Your Eyes Only

**Managing Muslims … like Bill Clinton? … prevention,
the best medicine … Malay affirmative action**

DR Mahathir is sometimes portrayed as nothing more than a
Machiavellian Muslim with an occasional mean streak.

That is just one of his obvious sides. It might not be the most
important. One quality alone, no matter how striking, does not
buy you 22 years in continuous power.

Obtaining power and maintaining power are not processes
associated with the nurturing of poets and philosophers. And
being out of power has necessarily lightened him up or rendered
him softer.

Let's be clear: Mahathir positively hates being out of power.
He probably even hates himself for being so big a fish so out of
water, flapping around for political air in the full open deck of
public opinion, worrying that someone bigger will sneak behind
and harpoon him in his gut.

Whatever his flaws, it's hard to imagine this man ever being
that much of a stiff. In the hours of interviews over four separate
days (and this is, relatively speaking, a lot of time), never did one
feel in the presence of an officious *official*. He felt like a real person,

a huge person, a complex person, a caring person, a worrisome person ... not some cipher.

Who does he remind me of most, of all those I've interviewed over the decades? For extemporaneous ad-lib talent: perhaps Bill Clinton. For seeming to be always at the near-edge of anger or extreme bluntness: perhaps Margaret Thatcher. For willingness to take a chance with a jab at wit or off-the-wall commentary and so the heck-with-it: Junichiro Koizumi.

Make no mistake about it: this former leader is no clown. As someone who somehow stayed at the top of the heap for 22 years in a country whose populace is 62 percent Muslim, a demographic not widely believed to be the easiest to govern, Mahathir's management style needs to be examined carefully.

I put that to him this way: "You know, my hope is that 50 years from now, someone will want to say, 'Well who was that Dr M?' and then pick up this particular book on you."

Mahathir looks at me as if to say, Dream On.

Or maybe he doesn't. So I take a chance and push forward, American-style (i.e., pushy), and suggest that, in order to secure our place in political literary history, we need a 'for-your-eyes-only' revelation ... like a big state secret.

He doesn't even tilt his head slightly. I'm not surprised but I am prepared. I brought with me—I'd been working on it for a few days—a little something that might be called a General Theory of (Mahathir's) Muslim Management. I just have to try it out; what can we lose?

Plunging onward: "There's an old device in English literature called 'The dog that didn't bark'. The idea is that what doesn't take place is sometimes more significant than what does take place. Here's what I mean…"

Dr M seems especially focused on me.

"During your 22 years in power, what do we see? A big tourist nightclub blows up, Australia, then another big terrorist blast in Bali, da-da, da-da, da-da, etc. Then the horrific downing of the twin towers of the World Trade Center, known as 9/11. And all over the world, including and especially Asia, almost everywhere, there is trouble … except in Malaysia. This is the country where nothing happens. NOTHING BAD HAPPENS LIKE ANY OF THESE THINGS THAT HAPPEN ELSEWHERE."

Dr M is staring at me and trying not to smile. But he looks very much like the proverbial cat that just swallowed a canary or two.

So what's the explanation? Is there an explanation?

He rubs a temple, studies me for a bit. Then his secretary appears at the door, says something in Malay, leaves. He picks up the phone, mumbles a few lines in Malay, puts the receiver down. He looks back at me, rubs the other temple, saying nothing. He wants me to continue.

Me continuing: "Now, maybe one can say, 'Well, Malaysians are just nice, quiet people; they don't do very much by way of violence.' 'Well, why would one say that?' 'Well, because they are quiet and don't do very much.' "

Funny, this sounds like a lame logical tautology to me.

Dr M isn't saying anything, but he is following me every word of the way. The beginning of a smile is spreading on the face of the Malay cat.

Plunging on: "So that cannot be the whole story! Maybe we need to go a bit deeper. What was it about Dr M's management of Malaysia, his government's management of the Muslims? They were responsible citizens."

He is quiet.

"Because, the last time I talked with you, I said, 'What is the one thing you are proudest of?' and you said, 'No explosion on my watch,' right? How did you do it? That's what I want to tell the Western world. Tell me how you did it. Give me your secrets!"

He took me seriously, and in fact I wasn't being at all facetious. For his 22 years at the helm, Malaysia was the very model of the dynamically growing Muslim country. I mean, if the place had been blowing up right and left every other month, wouldn't he get a lot of the blame? By the same logic, precisely because what happened was the direct opposite, shouldn't his generalship rate a gold star or two?

Mahathir is thinking all the while I am talking. He seems to be measuring his response, but then it seemed just to cascade out, almost casually.

Then it comes, but now almost a gusher: "Oh, you take early action. You do things before it happens. You know, a lot of things have been said against these preventive laws. But preventive laws are laws meant to prevent crimes, or whatever, from happening, because they are meant to deter people from doing something. A preventive law is much more activist than ordinary laws. I mean, if you see a man holding a knife and is about to stab somebody, you can act before he stabs somebody, because then it'd be a crime. Preventive law is like that. When you see people getting over-emotional in a multiracial country, you know that sooner, *and sooner rather than later*, they would be fighting each other. They would actually be killing each other, and this happened in 1969."

"Right."

"We learned a lesson from that. So, when you see people moving in that direction…"

"You move in."

Dr M is speaking with some feeling here: "…especially when they get very emotional, we have to put a stop to that. We have to act before that thing happens. Not often, but people usually respond to this thing, because in this country we value the security of the people rather more than the right of any individual."

"Hmm."

"But, of course, it must be a real fear that this thing is about to happen … then you can act. Well, in 1987 these things happened. Well, of course, it's the police who make the assessment. Maybe they are sometimes overzealous. In that case, I think they were. Even so, that [whole exercise] served as a reminder to people that if you breach the undertaking not to bring up emotional issues in a

multiracial country, then you might have to face the consequences."
[See previous story "The Men With the Golden Guns"]

A Mahathir Political Point
In a multiracial country the citizen's right
for totally free expression does not exist
—if you want a peaceful community.

Dr Mahathir is on a roll now. He then points out that there are always critics of this approach, inside Malaysia as well as in the West (though perhaps a little less so in the rest of Asia), who will complain: " 'Well, we should be more liberal,' they argue, and permit more discussion of controversial issues, like race relations, for example. The moment you do that, they go back. They go back to discussing this [kind of] thing and getting emotional, and getting angry with each other. And now [2010] we have become more separate than we were during the time when this was going on. During my time, people don't discuss, and therefore they don't get heated up."

Note that he is saying "*during my time*".

"So Malaysia is tensing up again?"

He nods. He swivels in his chair a little left and then right.

"You mean, you think there's more polarization now?"

"Yeah. Yes. More, much more."

"And, that's due to … why is that?"

"Well, because you allow people to talk. And, of course they will say things which will hurt the other side."

"And you didn't allow that."

On this point Dr M seems almost triumphant: "At that time we didn't allow that. You want to talk about these things, let's have a closed room, let the leaders talk, and you'll settle what it is you can do."

"But no rabble-rousing."

"No rabble-rousing, no demonstrations in the streets. You see what happened in Thailand? It started off with a very simple, gentle demonstration, and it ended up with many people being killed. And Bangkok being burned."

"Right."

"That's what happens."

I know my colleagues in the Western media will hate me for this but I plow on anyway: "That's where you and LKY look relatively good. You get people to come into Kuala Lumpur and see it's not burning; you go to Singapore and it's not burning. But people say, 'Oh, they're soft authoritarians.' Well, maybe there is a plus side to that? I mean, I know you both worry about the Gini coefficient, which measures income disparity in a country. You were always worried about that, right?"

Mahathir smiles and nods. He knows exactly what Gini is about. I bet a lot of leaders of failed or underperforming states do not. Malaysia, Singapore and almost everyone else has a Gini problem (the United States especially, Japan less so). But some governments don't even care that they do.

Me saying: "Gini is about the gap between the rich and the poor. Too much Gini can lead to political instability unless you impose severe political repression. So who was worrying about Gini in Thailand? Nobody in control was worrying apparently ... that's one big reason the place blew up."

My voice rises a bit here. I am not fond of *so-called* democratic systems that ignore the needs of everyone except central elites, any more than one admires authoritarian regimes that oppress the populace. They make me angry.

Dr M agrees: "The rural and the urban; the rich and the poor..."

"Right, I've got mine, and too bad for you. Thailand could blow up again. They didn't get a stable resolution, I don't think. So, the so-named 'Land of the Smiles' becomes the land of the cries, right?"

I catch my breath and realize I am straying far from Malaysia, though only a little bit northwards on the map, actually. The assumption that a political system is good simply because it is superficially democratic strikes me as ideological, if not hypocritical.

The point is to frame his job in a way with which he can relate, for the purpose of our continuing conversation, without ignoring the obvious ethical questions of critics.

"So many people think that what you did in helping keep multiethnic Malaysia together is fascinating and commendable. Not just the economic development part, which obviously speaks for itself. I mean, you arrive at the airport—it's fantastic! And this capital city's great. But some writers see Malaysia as little more than one big corruption country, and they see the dominant political party [UMNO] as just a big corruption machine. And they look at the 1987 crackdown not as a matter of maintaining public order but keeping UMNO at the top of the hill."

He is quiet.

I say to him: "I've been trying to imagine what it would be like to be you. The instinct comes from having done graduate work at Princeton in public policy. Policy schools teach you something quite different—that it's not easy to run a country. It's difficult. So some of my American colleagues think I'm too soft, in a way, on so-called 'soft authoritarianism'. Some people think I may have been too soft on LKY in the prior book ... I don't care. That book is what I think should have been written. Same with this one."

Dr M now is expecting the usual blast. It goes like this: Malaysia, an oil exporting country, was like a corrupt Third World country, the only difference being that, rather than being poor, increasingly it was becoming rich. But ethically it was no better.

It might be time to look at it with considerably more nuance.

Me continuing: "But I look at it this way. I figure UMNO as one of the ways that you control and manage society, and instead of using a negative word, we will use a term that the economists use—economic incentives. To get people to behave, you get them to buy into the system, literally as well as figuratively. You use positive economic incentives."

I can see he is following me closely.

I continue: "So, for example, look at what I call your program of 'affirmative action for the majority'. Now technically, it is NOT what Americans call affirmative action; in the States a relatively rich and powerful majority hand over educational and hiring concessions to the less fortunate. In Malaysia the majority ruling party [UMNO] aggregates to the Malay majority [about 62 percent] affirmative action-type advantages. Under the 'New Economic Policy' put in place years ago, the majority Malay gets preferences."

The arguments for this upside-down implementation of 'affirmative action for the majority' are perhaps two-fold. The first is economic: that without it, the Malays will struggle to climb any higher on the wage-earnings ladder, especially in competition with the Chinese.

The second is political: that if the majority Malay does not get at least a 62 percent slice of the pie (even if their work effort is not at the level), there will be political instability. This means that either the majority party, UMNO, will fall, or the 'ultra' Muslim religious party, PAS, will take over. Or (presumably) both.

PAS, by the way, had introduced Sharia law where its few political victories permitted. In the states of Kelantan and Terengganu, the hijab was mandatory on women. PAS, to be sure, is entitled to its views and its political program. But make no mistake about the direction it was headed and where it would wind up if it ever got total control of Malaysia.

During the Mahathir era the policy of trying to satisfy the Malay majority was refined, and mostly worked. But it may have planted the seeds of Malaysia's erosion. It has driven some of the best Chinese Malaysian citizens to seek to get on with their lives elsewhere; and the brain drain out of the country appears not to be abating.

And it may have had the unintended consequence of deepening the culture of Malay dependency on the government's preferential treatment. Rather than making Malays more muscular, it may have weakened their ability to compete, perpetuating the problem (spelled out by Mahathir himself in his seminal 1970 book, *The Malay Dilemma*). Recently, Dr M himself has admitted that a new Malay dilemma has arisen: the inability of Malays, as a culture, to throw away the crutches provided by government affirmative action over the decades and compete on their own two feet.

Perhaps a balanced view of Mahathir's Malay policy during his years in power would allow that no social policy is without its downside. The American public itself is usually deeply divided on the affirmative action approach in its own backyard. On taking power back in 1981, Mahathir, it seems to me, could come up with no other way out of 'The Malay Dilemma'. If there are serious problems with it, as there surely are, at least it did offer people who haven't been getting ahead a way to get ahead, and have a stake in the society.

In fact, one of Mahathir's undeniable achievements was getting the Chinese minority to buy into a system that in effect handicapped them.

I say: "And then you worked hard with the Chinese, who had felt that they were excluded from getting ahead, and you felt that at the end of the day, you had a good rapport with them; you had a pretty good feeling from them."

No doubt Mahathir's wooing of the Chinese sector of his country was precisely calculated to bolster the ruling coalition. But it worked economically. They were generally well integrated into the economy, and often served as political allies.

Now we move to a possible killer point: "So when you had to cope with PAS and they want to take an issue and make it a radical issue, I felt you Mahathirized them."

His eyes light up.

"You would take the issue away from them. You know what I mean? And, before you know it, boom! PAS had lost exclusive control of the issue. So in a way you remind me a little bit of Bill Clinton. You know, Republicans thought they could get Clinton on the welfare-reform issue, because there's those darn blacks and other minorities getting … you know, all that free stuff from government. But stealthily, Clinton stole welfare reform from them and made it his own issue. Before the Republicans knew it, boom, they had been Clintonized; they lost the issue. Fast Willy tricked them."

Me going on: "Now, when I use the word 'trick', I don't necessarily mean that in a negative way. Many so-called tricks are in fact clever skills of political management. One could regard a policy of targeted income redistribution as a primary method of social control."

Mahathir doesn't say anything, but he is following everything.

"Now I made my researcher My Lu laugh with this: I said, 'You know, in a way Dr M kind of bribed the whole country to behave!' Actually one admires that, because how in the heck else are you going to do it? You're going to arrest everybody? Follow everyone around? You're going to make it into a pure dictatorship? You have to have all these levers of control. So, I was hoping … could you critique my panoramic view and perhaps overly fanciful reconstruction of how you operated? Am I all wrong? Is it close?"

What has been put on the table is a little theory of what might be termed 'politically efficient corruption'. The concept may be worth considering carefully.

It would go something like this: economically speaking, the corrupt (or politically bent) distribution of resources is almost always inefficient; it almost has to be, from the emotionless logic of modern economics.

But is that assumption always the last word from the standpoint of running a country? For it may sometimes be the case that 'politically efficient corruption' produces something of value that cannot always be quantifiable: getting key elements of a society to buy into the system so as to attain political stability. This approach might not be the most economically equitable; but it may be the most politically efficient.

It seems like he waits a quarter of any hour, but probably it is only a few slower than the usual ticks of the clock.

Finally him responding: "I would say it [your outline] is close, because when you look after the welfare of people, and practically telling them that—'I will give you this if you behave'—then you are actually employing what is akin to bribery."

"Yes."

Then he rolls his head left and right and says: "But you must give people something. Either you use a big stick to hammer them the moment they get out of line, or you reward them. I prefer reward."

Yes, there's a reason or two he was elected five times, besides the obvious muscle of the dominant political party, UMNO. While increasing the size of the economic pie, he kept a lid on the place, while avoiding (at least by his own measurement, if not that of his critics) using the hammer as far as possible.

I continue: "Now, maybe this place doesn't have as many crazies as Indonesia, but it must have some. There must have been some risks, and some dangers, right? So to explain what you stood for, to Americans and Europeans, we have to explain to them that the management of a multiracial country that is predominantly Muslim is not easy. It takes a lot of different things."

He huddles at his desk like an owl looking over everything,

almost consciously slowing himself down, as if trying to decide where to go with a point that somehow troubles him. Suddenly he doubles back to the management of a Muslim country theme that he discussed earlier. He reminds me of his view that wholly secular standards of achievement (even arguably spectacular ones) will not suffice to legitimize a government when important religious-related questions arise—as they inevitably will.

Please note that Dr Mahathir is not talking about governing Turkey, with its forced determination over many decades to steer governance in a strictly secular direction, but about his Malaysia, a country whose culture places a premium on religious belief and ritual. Here, he is saying, governance that only offers secular policy-type or legalistic reasons for what it does and what its people must do governs only superficially at best.

That, it could be argued, was the mistake of the Shah's Iran, whose excessive secularity ushered in the "purifying" 1979 Islamic Revolution. One senses that Dr M figured out early on that one sure way of becoming (in effect) an ousted Shah would be to go into denial and try to ignore the deep religious forces in his country that make it, well, Malaysia.

But leaving aside this vital exception, the secular dimension of governance did otherwise require entirely secular-style calibrations. By itself, a purely religious approach wouldn't have worked either.

So I bring him back to the 'politically efficient corruption' theme: "And so, if we put this all together, you think we've got it close?"

He nods.

"Alright, because I'm going to go with that."

He says: "I think it's as near as you can get."

Is he just being polite?

I press it a little: "Anything else you want to add? Have I forgotten anything or left something out?"

"Nothing."

I have only pressed this point because Dr M, as stated at the very beginning of the book, is a fox, not a hedgehog. He is clever at surviving in very many ways. But some of his tactical instincts, if stitched together in some more formal way, become almost hedgehog-like. Not that he knows it, of course.

Or, for that matter, particularly cares.

A Mahathir Political Point
There's nothing like an ounce of harsh prevention, because it's a lot better than a lot of so-called liberal cure.

The Mother Who Loved Me

**Mom was the big influence … women's growing role
… what he believes … the Dirty Hands problem**

POLITICAL leaders tend not to be big fans of personal
psychoanalysis. They figure it's for marginal characters—for the
weak-minded, the crib-coddled, the royally spoiled. You wouldn't
have gotten Winston Churchill within an empty brandy bottle of
a shrink's couch. Even Gandhi, for all his pacifism, wouldn't have
been caught dead curled up on a leather sofa, babbling on about
mother and various childhood experiences.

But towering political figures that might seem too good to be
true … or too bad to be real … might benefit from indulging us,
at least, with some introspection. Nudging them to talk a bit about
past influences can humanize them whether they want to appear
human or not.

I knew Macho Mahathir, for one, wouldn't be eager to slip
onto the couch and dig down deep into his psyche about his
family. But I also figured that if I raise the issue early enough in our
conversations, he wouldn't want to seem uncooperative, and in fact
might calculate that he might as well dispose of the subject sooner
rather than later.

I figure it is best to get to it before losing the chance. So I let fly…

"Would you be okay talking about the impact on your ambitions of your mother and your father?"

He seems grumpy, and his deep-set, rotund eyes roll just a bit.

"What was your family like?"

Another pause but now he does answer.

"Yeah. Okay. They obviously brought me up and instilled values in me and taught me right from wrong, and my faith in my religion and all that—that was my parents. But my father was great on education. In the days when Muslims refused to go to English schools, because the English schools were run by missionaries and the missionaries were of course interested in conversion, he went to school. He went without telling his parents. He practically ran to the school. He was so keen on education."

"How did education change his life?"

"Well, obviously because of his qualifications, he had more opportunities open to him and he was invited to the state of Kedah. He was from Penang Island. He went to Kedah because he was invited to start an English school for royalty. He was the first headmaster of the school. He was a founder of the school, actually. So all his life he's been keen that his children should get a good education. He was very keen on what we call English education, because during the British period they set up schools where the medium of teaching was English. So all his children, he sent to the English school."

"I see, so who was the stronger figure in your life—your mother or your father?"

"My mother."

"Why? What was she like?"

"She was more with me than my father."

"Why, father was out a lot?"

"He was working."

"Did that closeness influence your attitudes toward the role of women in Malaysia? Against the backdrop of what we in the West expect from a Muslim culture, they may not be what every Western feminist would prefer, but they are more progressive than perhaps expected. One figure I saw was that more than 50 percent of your women are working women. I don't know if that's true."

"Yeah, it is." No question, there's pride in his voice.

He didn't want to discuss it, but no doubt a further point of pride in the 'women's-liberation' category is his impressive daughter, Marina Mahathir. This woman has become a one-lady feminist movement in Malaysia, tackling with courage tough social issues such as AIDS awareness and Islamic violence. When in early 2010 a string of Christian churches in Malaysia were firebombed, her denunciations of the brutal arsonist attacks practically forced the feeble federal government in Kuala Lumpur to wake up and do something about them. She claimed violence was not the Islamic way—and, in this respect, her views echo those of her father.

But even if Marina is far ahead of Dad, Dad is not exactly a deadhead on the issue. Note that about 60 percent of Malaysia's computer industry's employees are women. Mahathir can hardly grab all the credit, but undoubtedly his government's emphatic prioritization of the technology sector (such as the bombastic but seriously progressive 'Multimedia Super Corridor' program and so on) helped. It dynamited holes through the old economy and created new vistas for Malaysian women. The impact on women's occupational options in that society was, whatever the motive, phenomenal.

Me asking: "You practically put a bomb under the old structure of the economy. Was that economic necessity? Or a touch of Western feminism somewhere in your Islamic soul? Is it both?"

He gives that cat smile again but answers in a serious way, giving a lot of the credit to Malaysian women themselves: "The upward movement of women is almost cultural. In the villages, for example, the women are the ones who do the rice planting. In the marketplace, for example, most of the people who are selling produce there are women, and now we are finding that more and more women are educated. In the universities, 60 percent of the students would be women."

I knew that women were attracted to higher education because it leads to positive steps up the economic ladder, but that figure struck me as high.

He continues: "No, it's 60 to 70 percent. There are instances where there are 70 percent and even more, and they are now better qualified, holding posts … which creates a social problem because they cannot find a spouse."

This rings a bell with me. One sees that all over rising affluent Asia: super-smart Asian women who (sometimes) tend to scare the living daylights out of traditional men, some of whom, for their part, prefer to view women as domestic acquisitions (like a living-room furniture set) than co-equal life partners.

You have to wonder how hard Mother Mahathir pushed her ambitious son, the oldest of the family litter.

"What were her values? What did she want for you?"

"She wants me to be a good boy…"

We both laugh.

"…and observe all the religious teachings and not do things which are wrong, not take things that do not belong to me, and things like that."

"How have you done?" I kind of josh him a little, I guess.

"Mm?"

"How have you done by her?"

"I think I have been quite ideal to most of her teachings, except…"

"What?" Big revelation here?

"She told me when I was a boy that there are two professions that I shouldn't take up. One is becoming a doctor, and the other one is a police inspector."

Oh, well… "Do not?"

"Do not take up these, because you'll get no sleep…"

We both laugh.

"…but I became a doctor."

I say: "Well, gee, like in the Korean community and other Asian communities here in the States, to be a doctor would be almost to be God! Did her attitude change when you became a doctor?"

"Well, when I got a scholarship to study medicine, she didn't object."

"So, then you were a practicing physician for 20 years, and we talked about that yesterday. At what point did you get the itch to be a politician?"

"I like to tell people I was a politician who became a doctor. I was involved in politics first. While in school, I was already leading groups of people in anti-British demonstrations and things like that, but being very young, people didn't take me seriously. So, I thought that if I get a university qualification, maybe then people would respect me, and heed what I tell them. So, that's why I wanted to become … go to university, or to study law."

The fact that Dr Mahathir's education was in English schools rather than Malay schools is significant. It internationalized his perspective, and left him with a reluctant respect for that culture even when he was happily bashing London (such as his semi-hilarious but effective 'Buy British Last' campaign, which he threw in the face of the Brits just three months after being PM).

"Right. So you wanted to be a professional of any sort, and you chose being a doctor."

"Not chose so much as, uh…"

Right, he grabbed what was offered: "The scholarship…"

"I had the opportunity to study medicine. In those days you don't ask too many questions; if you are offered something, you just take it."

"And did you have the aptitude for science?"

"Yeah, I discovered that I liked science. Of course, it undermined my faith at one stage, but I got over it."

All religions require acts of faith on the part of their adherents that defy reason, of course. It's almost impossible to believe that a man as carefully calculating and scientifically inclined could trust any religion at all.

Me saying: "Not too long ago the previous Catholic Pope wrote about faith and reason, and he said that while you must respect reason, and take reason as far as you can go with it, at some point reason won't give you all the answers, and then that's where faith kicks in. So his argument was that it wasn't in contradiction but that the relationship of faith and reason was symbiotic. Do you buy that?"

That catches the good doctor's intellectual fancy. The scientist in him works his way from the comforts of a fact-based universe to the irresistible human fascination with the inexplicable.

This is what he says: "Well, I reasoned things out, and finally I came to the conclusion that where science can answer the question 'How', it cannot answer the question 'Why'. So, when you come to the question 'Why' you have to attribute it to something that you don't understand. You can call it Nature, if you like, but when you ask 'What is Nature?' there is no explanation."

The question raised is whether knowledge stops where science stops.

I ask: "So when you were into science, it began to raise questions about God, critical questions, secular questions. How long did it take you to reconcile it, or haven't you reconciled it?"

Mahathir taking his time answering … then: "I was confused for quite some time, but actually after studying science and asking questions, I discovered that every time you ask 'Why' they answer 'How'. They say that this is *how* things happen, they're not telling me *why* things happen. You see, I began to ask myself a lot of questions, for example, why is it that you breathe in oxygen and you live? Why not nitrogen? Why not chlorine? There's no answer. Had God made you breathe in chlorine, you wouldn't ask any more questions, you would say, 'Of course you must breathe in chlorine to live.' But this is oxygen we breathe. And they explain to you how it gets oxidized in the body and comes out as carbon dioxide and things like that, but *why*?"

"Yeah, that's not the question you asked. Why is it oxygen? Why not something else?"

The scientist in him knows how oxygen is used, but the philosopher in him wonders why we humans wound up as oxygen breathers. And the Muslim in him suspects a providential role that no mere scientist can begin to explain.

Dr M adding, and here he seems a bit intense: "Actually, you should become an even stronger believer if you are a scientist, because now you know that everything is made up of very tiny atoms, made up of electrons and protons and things like that. Everything is made up of that. Why? So tiny, and yet the universe is so huge. I mean, at the time of the Prophet, if he had preached that the universe is so huge that it would take many light years for you to travel from one star to another, they would call him mad and they would never have accepted his teachings. But we know now that the universe is so huge that it is unimaginable."

This seems a side of Dr M not many have seen.

"Why? I mean, where are these stars? So, there is a black hole, a big bang and things like that, but why? You still can't answer."

To get Dr M back down to earth, I tried to get the prophet in him back to Malaysian ground level: "So, now here's a *why* question, and the *why* question is the question of evil, and the question of the eight-year-old child who has cancer, terminal cancer. Or consider the question of a tsunami that wipes out a tenth of Indonesia or whatever. In the Mahathir universe, is there room for the Devil? Does that help us understand things, or is that a little too hocus-pocus?"

People who think politicians are themselves evil incarnate might be surprised to learn that the concept of evil is something that can also preoccupy them.

He says: "For me, the Devil is ... if you think of being good, and then you get some kind of well, shall we say [supportive] message or something like that? But that we should then think: why not do something bad? These are conflicts in your mind. I don't think of the Devil as some creature that you cannot see that's hovering around or anything like that. I think that there is an evil influence around us and it affects us."

A Mahathir Political Point

Figuring out how something works is the easy part; understanding why anything works the way it does may be beyond human understanding. Faith can help get you over it. And it's ultimately humbling.

Mahathir never encountered formal training in political philosophy, but he never had to, of course. He lived the hard real life of a Muslim Machiavelli, having to do real things on this planet Earth in real time. Accordingly, he is no stranger to the moral dilemma of Dirty Hands: this means having to commit some obvious wrong for the public good (assassinate a terrorist suspect who is believed to be a suicide bomber before he arrives at the crowded church, for example).

So here goes—the university professor in me: "Right. But the evil question is an easier question for a cleric, or an imam, or a priest, or a cardinal. But for a head of state or for a prime minister, the evil question is a tough one because sometimes, under the time-honored Doctrine of Dirty Hands, the Prince sometimes has to do something dirty for a good reason. How did you deal with that when you were a prime minister for 22 years? You had to make tough decisions. So did you say to yourself, 'Am I doing this because I'm evil, or am I doing this because in the final analysis, the end does justify the means?' "

From the way he's delaying his answer, his face reflecting puzzlement but probably not irritation, he seems to treat it as a fair but not easy topic of reflection.

"Well, you have to struggle with such a question, but when you want to do something for the country and you are opposed, well you can get evil thoughts—'I wish that he'd be quiet' or 'I wish I could throw him in jail' and things like that. To me, that is evil. But it wasn't really necessary; I had to survive in a system that depends upon popularity."

"Right."

But people were thrown in jail from time to time, if allegedly for violations of national-security law or (in the case of Anwar) for alleged sexual violations.

Dr M adding: "You see, I can go this far and not beyond that. I go too much … I do something I think is good but people think is bad, then I will just lose my position."

Me saying: "Right … now here's sort of a dumb question but I'm never afraid to ask a dumb question, because I know your answer won't be dumb. But, if you're in KL, and you see a Muslim woman in black except for the slits for the eyes and you know it's 95 degrees out, and then you see the man with her, and he's, sensibly, in a T-shirt … I mean, couldn't they come up with a lighter outfit in the desert? Isn't this a kind of evil against women?"

The thing about Dr M, when you confront him with reality,

is that he rarely goes into denial.

He says: "This also happened to Christianity before, the way you treat women. In the past, they were not equal to you. And you say, well, women cannot go to Cambridge University. They cannot learn anything about religion even, or to become doctors. I read this book by Ken Follett and he was saying that this woman was very clever, very good, she was a nun, she wanted to study medicine, but she was too low [in society's pecking order]. Women cannot study medicine. So this discrimination against women is everywhere. Of course we see a lot of intolerance in other places, but the women with the covered faces, they're not Malays. They're not Malaysian. They are Arabs."

"I see."

"They come here as tourists."

"Is that right? They're all tourists?"

"Actually, it is against the teaching of Islam. In the Quran, it says clearly, you must keep your face open; you must keep your hands uncovered."

"Is this the Saudi Arabian sect? Wahhabis?"

"Yeah, Saudi Arabians, Afghans and—"

"Are the Saudi Arabians proselytizing here in Malaysia?"

"Um, well, they're not ... well-accepted."

"Is that right?"

"Yeah, we belong to the Sunni sect, Shafie school, and they are Wahhabis and they are…"

"Not getting very far?"

"Not getting very far, no."

"Do you allow them to proselytize or—"

"Yeah, we allow them."

"Do you have to watch them a little bit?"

He doesn't answer that, but everyone knows his internal security police kept a watch out on many activities and population segments during his 22 years. He probably knows what's going on even now but isn't telling me.

He says: "We do have a few such [*motions his hand over his face signifying a cover*] Malays, but they find that wearing black is something that they don't like. You see them wearing the colored *tudung* [head scarf]."

"Yeah, it's lovely."

"And they truly do look prettier and the focus is on the face."

It's fair to say that Dr M might actually be a fairly keen observer of the female gender—and good for him! So I ask whether competing Malaysian mores might be confusing for a young Malay teenager growing up in a society of veils, on one hand, and mass-entertainment figures (like Beyoncé, her international tour once contemplating a Kuala Lumpur show stop).

"I think we have all kinds of people here. It's not everybody who is wearing veils. In any case, they expose their faces. But here we have people wearing mini-skirts, and we have people wearing veils. We are very lax about this; we don't insist. If you go to Saudi Arabia, you have to cover up, but here, you are a foreigner, you have your own way of dressing. That's okay. We are quite relaxed because we live in this country, a multiracial country, multireligious country—not only recently, it has been a long time. We know that people are different."

"But isn't there one predominant way? I mean, we tolerate every religion in America, but we've never had a Jewish president. You know what I mean? I understand that there is a lot of tolerance, but isn't there one kind of predominant culture?"

"I think that because it is a Muslim-majority country, if Beyoncé comes here, she's expected to dress a little bit more well, uh ... yeah, cover up a little bit more. But beyond that it's alright. There will be these extremist people who will say, 'Well, she shouldn't be allowed here' but the majority? We are okay, because we have 60 percent Muslim and 40 percent non-Muslim. We have places where you have a church here, and a mosque here, and a Hindu temple there. This is something that has been going on for a long time. We are used to it."

Malaysia inherited some good things from British colonialization, such as a widespread bilingualism that includes the international language of business—English. But as a long-colonized region—once under the protection of China, then taken over by the Portuguese, then the Dutch (1641) and finally the British (1825-1957)—the Malays never had control of their destiny until the relatively recent watershed of independence.

Dr M amplifying: "One of the problems we had was that under the British, we were separated ... the Indians in the rubber estates, the Chinese in the cities and towns, and the Malays in the paddy fields, rice fields. But now we have to bring them together because we cannot have this division, and that's still very difficult."

In fact, Dr M's critics argue that his persistence with affirmative action for the majority Malays had the unintended effect of reasserting Malay ethnic identity and encouraging Malay clustering across the board of that increasingly divided culture.

Mahathir won't deal with that but moves to another point: "I feel if they come to town from the country, and they accept the people in the town are dressed that way, so be it. It's quite alright. If your daughter were living here, I am quite sure she will enjoy living here. I have met lots of European girls who come here. Of course, some of them are a little bit wild—we cannot tolerate such behavior—a little bit free with themselves, but otherwise they will find life here quite acceptable."

"So you're not worried about our Western ways!"

"No, no."

Quantum of Solace

**Drug use and legalization? … mental health …
family ties … old-age homes as cultural indicators**

No truly modern nation can stay afloat for long in an isolation tank. Even Singapore (a proud, almost classic island nation-state) was among the first to accept that extreme *inter*dependence was not just a luxury but also a survivalist necessity.

But the price of global networking is not zero. Reaching out means no longer being able to stay within oneself. That can lead to identity issues.

Malaysian culture is as rich as any and Malays are as proud of their culture as anyone. But the times are changing for the land of the Malays as for almost everyone on the face of the earth.

Like most true patriots, Mahathir is wistful about his country's cultural values, more than a few of which he fondly wishes would remain eternally valid. He finds in the magic of family loyalty the ultimate bulwark against street homelessness, and the iron hand of firm government the best antidote to drug use. But in Malaysia, as elsewhere, family bonds are weakening, and the iron fist of Malay culture and the law are losing their grip on limiting drug usage.

Yet as we talk about such prevalent social issues, the former

PM shows a yearning for the past that doesn't quite square with the image of the pragmatic policy progressive. We start with the notion (my wholly unsolicited opinion) that government efforts to criminalize drug use are successful only at filling up jails, not eliminating drug use. I find it an anomaly that Mahathir—a physician who should know better—should toe the war-on-drugs hard line.

He answers me by putting the drug-use issue into an historical and contemporary perspective.

"Well, during the period when we were under British rule, opium was a [colonial] government monopoly. The licensed opium smokers were really old people ... old people, workers who need to, well, relax in a way. So this drug taking without a license is a new phenomenon for us, new in the sense that it happened after we became independent. And this really is the byproduct of the general usage of drugs in other parts of the region. The drugs pass through Malaysia from the Golden Triangle and all that, and as they pass through Malaysia ... they [drug dealers] have used methods which are so very unacceptable. You know, like getting children to sell drugs, or to smuggle drugs."

"Here in Malaysia?"

"Here in Malaysia, yes, so much so that we have to be very severe. We have the death penalty for smuggling drugs or distributing drugs. And people say that this is draconian, that in these days you don't have to have capital punishment. But if you look at the people who have suffered as a result of drug taking, you will understand how seriously we feel about drug taking. So, that is why the penalty is very, very severe."

"Well, in that respect it's one of the areas where you agree with Singapore."

"Yes, yes."

"I remember Lee Kuan Yew was once asked on American television if he thought capital punishment for drug dealers was too severe, and he said, 'I only wish I could execute them 80 times over.' "

Mahathir shakes his head and smiles at that: "Yeah, but this … the situation is much worse in Malaysia already."

"Because you're bigger?"

"Yes, much bigger."

"The only reason it's worse in Malaysia?"

He shakes his head: "And we have a lot of young people who are not very well brought up, and they are very prone to this … to accepting this habit. You see, we lose them. Once they're on drugs, we lose them."

"It's hard to get them off it once they're on it."

"We have treatment centers all over that cost the government a lot of money, but the moment they are cured, we send them back and they go back to the same habit. So you see, it's a very serious problem for us."

I try this on him: "There was a famous American opinion columnist who died not long ago named William F. Buckley, Jr. … very conservative. But he decided that the punitive law-enforcement approach to drug control just was not working, and that it wasn't ever going to work. He said you have to treat it as a disease, and the best thing to do would be to legalize and then regulate it. And then after the government regulates it, you thus control it, and that way you wouldn't have the drug mafias, and you wouldn't have all the potential corruption of your police. That is to say, deal with it as a medical issue rather than as a law enforcement issue. What do you think?"

He shakes his head and gruffly says: "It's not going to work." He says this with unusual emphasis.

"Not going to work?"

"As long as there are drugs available, as long as you allow people to grow opium or cocaine, then you are going to have drug addiction. Law enforcement needs to, of course, try to eliminate drug sources in whatever way it can."

I note *"in whatever way it can"*.

So I pitch another very thorny medical/social-policy question to our sometimes not-so-soft soft authoritarian: "In some cultures drug users are stigmatized as nothing more than criminals; stigmatization of mental-health patients is also commonplace. With a doctor as head of the government for more than two decades, is the Malaysian view more nuanced?"

"It's difficult to define mental health now, because there are the mild ones and there are the extreme ones. Then you see a man who is about to walk naked in the street, and you know he's not quite there. But on the other hand, there are some people with mild schizophrenia, for example … you don't notice it. We worry about these things. We have treatment centers for them, but with extreme cases, we have not been able to cure them in any way. Some cases now respond to drugs. Then they become calm and then they behave normally. So, we don't look down upon them or anything but—"

"You do not?"

Here he seems extremely self-assured: "No, we don't, but we think that they need treatment. The government gives free medicine to the whole country, and people who are insane, the government has to confine them to asylums and places like that, and provide them with treatment."

In America prescription drug-abuse may be as much of a social problem as illegal narcotic use.

Me saying: "In America there seems now to be a drug for almost anything. If you're blue, there's an anti-blue drug; if you're too happy there's an anti-too-happy drug. Is this phenomenon purely an example of excessive affluence and conspicuous consumption, or is it the march of science? Are a lot of these things really things that can be controlled, and should be controlled? Or are we in a new era?"

"I admit it's much more difficult to control now than it was before. But in America you're generally very liberal. We're not as liberal but of course in America there are certain drugs … psychotropic drugs, you know drugs that are supposed to calm you down and enable you to sleep; these are too easily available, and everybody has a drug for everything."

"Of course, in America too, you know, some of the doctors are part of the problem. Some are promiscuous prescription drug pushers. But in this era of sexual promiscuity and, for instance, mandated inoculations for STDs and so on, can Muslim doctrines of abstinence prevail, or is it a losing battle?"

He shakes his head: "Yeah, I think we maybe are better off, perhaps, than more liberal countries. The religious restraint is there, but I think we are slowly sliding, and it's very difficult to fight."

He's right, no nation is an island: "Is that creeping permissiveness part of the cost of globalization and the availability of alternative symbols and images of authority?"

It's obvious he has thought about the issue a lot: "All kinds of things happening in other parts of the world are very corruptly shown, and with that, there's no doubt that we are influenced. Our values change, especially among the more impressionable younger people."

"And what can be done about it … nothing?"

"Uh, it's very difficult now. You cannot censor anything, especially the Internet. There's no way you can do it because they can gain access somehow."

"Now, is Malaysia becoming more like the U.S.?"

"Well, more like the West, not just the U.S. Promiscuity is not as widespread, but we see a lot babies being thrown into rubbish heaps and things like that."

"Really?" Malaysia strikes me as anything but a perfect place, but, in some respects, far less imperfect than some.

"Yes, but before that there was none."

"Never happened, right?"

"Yeah."

"How about homelessness? How much of that do you have here and what do you do about it?"

"Not so much. I mean, you walk the streets of Malaysia's towns and cities, you don't see the kind of beggars, smelly people who really never bathe at all, as I saw when I was in the U.S."

"Why is that? Why do you have less here? Because you don't have as much money as we do?"

"I think the family ties are still there. There is a sense of shame if members of your family have become beggars ... except for those who really have no family, but that is very rare. You know, our policy is not to give unemployment benefits. We want the families to look after the unemployed. They become so ashamed of being unemployed, I mean, to sponge on their family, that they would rather go and work."

"Do anything, almost."

"Do anything to earn something for themselves, rather than be dependent."

"So, in some ways you think the social safety net is counter-productive."

"There was a lot of abuse of the so-called social safety net."

"So, the Asian way is, rely on the family and get a job."

"Yeah. Even the family, the extended family, want to still

continue this. This split up the nuclear family, husband and wife, or even single mothers and all that … this kind of neglect is not really acceptable in Malaysia."

"On the other end of the timeline, in America, across the country, senior citizen homes and retirement homes and so forth are a big industry. Do you have a lot of that here?"

"We're beginning to see some, but I'm shocked, because I wouldn't think that I would send some old members of my family to stay and die in a home away from the family. Normally, we try to look after our old people. We try to give them loving care until their last days."

"That's still the Malaysian tradition?"

"Yes, especially for the Muslims. For the Chinese, a lot of them prefer to send [the elderly] to old peoples' homes and things like that."

"Is that a cultural difference, or is it the money?"

"It is a cultural difference."

"It is kind of god-awful when you think about it."

"Yes."

A Mahathir Political Point

**Cultural restraints against serious
deviation becomes less effective
when the culture itself is changing.**

Goldfinger

Going Hollywood ... the audacity of defiance ... the Asian Financial Crisis ... Western collapse

PUT the label 'Western' on almost anything and Dr M's marvelous (if sometimes obvious) putdown machine goes into full gear.

Western journalists? Superficial, ideological, Godless. Western politicians? Spineless, generally; too pro-Israel, usually; parochial, often enough.

These generalizations entertain imaginations all across Asia, of course, not just among Malays. And, to be sure, like almost any broad assertions, they contain a measure of truth to them.

But it is also true that what no well-balanced Malay, including Mahathir, can deny is that Malaysia needs the West—and especially the United States—to gobble up its goods, help educate its young people, provide a plausible military counterweight to a rising China (should it head off in an unexpected bad direction), and of course provide endless fresh, funny fodder for its Malaysian comediennes, professional or otherwise.

The latter comment is not intended to suggest that Malaysian culture lacks the capacity for self-examination. Countless blogs criticize almost all things Malaysian, often including even Dr M himself. Books (such as the delightful *Honk, If You're Malaysian*, by Lydia Teh) make light fun of national habits.

At the same time, some unquantifiable segment of its society still regard the country's most famous former PM as an incomparable figure. Nothing else could explain "Mahathir, the Musical", a two-hour theatre extravaganza that in the fall of 2010 opened for a short run in Kuala Lumpur, and was so popular that the run was extended. But it probably won't make it to Broadway, for better or for worse.

But undoubtedly, Dr M's place on the Malaysian stage is secure. One reason is the widespread memory of his sheer audacity.

People understood, for example, that his capacity for knocking the U.S. was exceeded only by his shamelessness about knocking on the door of U.S. money-men (some of them Jewish!) when a pet project needed to be pitched. In fact, it was on just such a money safari that I first observed the then-PM in audacious action. This was in January 1997, when I interviewed him in a snug but comfortable bungalow at the swank Beverly Hills Hotel for my Asia column, then running in the *Los Angeles Times*.

Mahathir was in town to hit up Hollywood's big-buck investors for his vaunted 'Multimedia Super Corridor' project. This was a grandiose plan for an intensive information-technology special development swath in Malaysia. The aim was to jump into the information age, much like Dr M sought to jump-start the national car industry with Proton. Presenting himself in a Western business suit, Mahathir was in top form as he pitched a kind of Southeast Asian Silicone Valley project at my readers.

As a columnist, I was not at all unhappy to try to help—economic development in general being a Basic Good Cause. And the next day's column, it seemed, was largely helpful. He made the project sound like a great idea.

The column did mention his much-noted edifice complex—the world's tallest two towers, the world's longest building—and the upcoming world's largest airport. And it did make the point that for all his bashing of the West's materialism and secularism, his was the first hand out when the boy needs dough. As he told me then: "If you can't fight them, you join them. You cannot avoid Hollywood. That's why we're here."

The Multimedia Super Corridor project got off to a good start. Hollywood, for all its alleged Jewishness, generally welcomes money-making proposals from all quarters—Muslim, Arab, who cares?—and regardless of race, creed, color or domestically-required political demagoguery.

Mahathir came across on that trip as an entertaining synthesis of an Asian Lawrence of Arabia and a Muslim Shylock.

But then came the summer of that same year and the Asian Financial Crisis. It was to knock the stuffing out of all grand schemes in Asia. The crisis rocked the value of many major Asian currencies, and took the air out of their stock markets. Some Asian leaders, notably sprawling Indonesia and industrializing South Korea, accepted Western bailout money from the International Monetary Fund and the World Bank. Both had their headquarters in Washington, if you get the idea.

The idea that the prime minister of Malaysia quickly got from their specific location and general policy outlook was that the Washington-dominated West was not to be trusted with organizing Asia's recovery. It was inclined to impose, on all troubled economies (no matter what their particular stage of development, political instabilities, cultural values or special needs), classical belt-tightening medicines right out of the basic playbook of liberal open-market economics.

Some of us were to depict this approach as narrow-minded free-market fundamentalist evangelicalism (at its most poisonous) because, like all fundamentalisms, the cause was always just, no matter the harm created while getting there.

When 1999 came and the Asian Financial Crisis was winding down, the political landscape of Asia had been dramatically altered. Totally upended, for instance, was the long-running General Suharto, who had run Indonesia, the world's largest Muslim country, for more than three decades.

But some leaders survived, in Singapore and elsewhere; but perhaps the survivor who stood tallest at the top of the heap—if only for the obvious success and audacity of his defiance—was Dr Mahathir.

As I wrote in August 1999 in my *Los Angeles Times* column "Asia Seeks Its Own Path to Globalization":

"There's more than one way to survive a crisis. It was about a year ago that two Southeast Asian economies ignored the

West's advice, introduced strikingly unorthodox measures to protect their fast-weakening currencies and roiling economies and triggered a transpacific diplomatic storm. The West, especially America, howled—as if, profanely, some sacred religious commandment had been violated.

But that did not stop Hong Kong from shoring up its stock market in an unprecedented way, and Malaysia from erecting a defiant firewall to protect its besieged currency from being speculated upon by craven outside interests.

What happened next was the stuff of regional legend: the unprecedented moves actually worked, and the West's unease at such economic unorthodoxy, aimed at Western stock and currency speculators, looks in retrospect suspiciously overwrought. Happy anniversary, Hong Kong and Malaysia. It looks like you were right and the West was wrong.

Hong Kong's Chief Executive Tung Chee-hwa never quite got fair credit from the local or international media, not to mention from the Hong Kong public, for the ingenuity and indeed courage of his government in fighting off the vast Western investment funds that prowled the Asian financial landscape in search of wounded economies—or economies it could wound.

Mahathir, however, did, precisely because this was one jungle lion that would not keep quiet at every turn. The way he paraded—if not flaunted—his combative agenda on behalf of the Malaysian national interest during that period reminded one of a Shakespearean line from *Henry V*: "In peace there's nothing that so becomes a man as modest stillness and humility; but when the blast of war blows in our ears, then imitate the action of the tiger...."

Wounded by the winds of the financial wars wafting across the region, Mahathir didn't wimp. He roared. He not only made speculation against the Malaysian national currency impossible to do, he made a noisy show of defying everyone in the West who said either (a) it couldn't be done or (b) if it could, it would be a tragic mistake.

And except for *New York Times* columnist Paul Krugman and a very few others, including myself, that's what everyone more or less said.

And most everyone turned out to be wrong.

The Mahathir roar had two levels of outrage, and in a sense they were contradictory rather than complimentary.

One was that the predatory Western hedge funds and stock- and currency 'shorting' raids that swept through Asia like locusts looking for crops to devour could not help themselves from eating away everything in sight. This is the Asian Islamic critique of the allegedly amoral Western economic system critique that forswears obnoxious profits for profits' sake alone.

But then there were the ad hominen and racial attacks: first against George Soros, the global financial figure, who (conveniently for pandering Muslim politicians) happened to be Jewish; and then against an overweening alleged Jewish conspiracy which through these destabilizing Western funds had taken deadly aim at Islamic economies.

We will see Dr M expound on these views in detail later.

His short-term perspective was that his nation and others in Asia (such as Islamic Indonesia) were targeted precisely because they were Islamic (rather than, crudely put, because they were ripe for the picking—which surely was the case).

But—longer term—what Mahathir took away from that ground-shaking experience in the late 90s was not simply fodder for the nationalist 'us-against-them' posturing options. It left him with the sincere conviction that Americans might be in truly serious trouble if in order to maintain their hefty and over-the-top lifestyle, economic 'Pearl-Harbor'-style sneak attacks against weaker economies had to be organized and mounted, almost in Crusade-style fashion.

Note that the old Asian view of America was as the more or less gentle hegemon, remarkably not seeking overt territorial empire in Asia after its crushing defeat of Japan. Now there was an emerging new view: that America seemed to have morphed into a seriously overweight animal on voracious prowl for any piece of meat that would get it through until the next meal.

In his office in the Perdana Leadership Foundation in Putrajaya, Dr M, dressed up in a brown Western-style sports coat, white shirt and pink-and-white striped tie, sought to describe what ails the world economy. (This was in September 2009, when the Obama administration was proclaiming a recovery that seemed curious for its failure to generate new jobs.)

I open this way: "Going back to when you put up the gates on your currency and brought your currency back home, the Western media criticized you, 'Terrible, terrible, terrible.' But you were right; those moves saved your economy from further exploitation. You knew exactly what you were doing and who the enemies were, and now, here it is ten years later in the United States, and look ... we kind of got bitten by our own mosquitoes! You must look at it with a certain degree of, well, look who's in trouble now, right?"

He smiles the cat-like grin: "These are huge mosquitoes, by comparison, to those mosquitoes which bit us."

I ignore that for the moment: "But you must look at it with a certain amount of amusement ... that we're getting kind of a dose of our own medicine?"

"It's always fun to watch that!"

We both laughed.

But here is where the laughing stopped: "Do you see the current financial crisis as one we're going to pull out of pretty soon, or are we stuck with it for a while?"

"You are going to live with it forever."

"Really?"

"As we are. Malaysia has not recovered."

"It's not recovered?"

"It's not recovered. And, whatever we do, the effect of this currency crisis will still be there, and the same thing is going to happen to the U.S., you see, because the so-called 'high per capita income' of the U.S. is not real. [The alleged] high per capita income consists of both real business but also fiddling around with the money."

Like a classic economic purist—or an Islamic banker— Mahathir views exotic forms of modern finance as deceptions and manipulations, rather than as objective derivatives from real wealth. But I'd never heard the phrase "fiddling around with the money before", and I frankly found its directness charming.

"This *what?*"

"This fiddling around with the money ... that 40 percent of the contribution to the American wealth comes from fiddling with the money. You see, those hedge funds, currency trading, sub-prime mortgages—all these things. These are not real business; they don't produce any goods, they don't employ anybody and they contribute nothing. They give no service to anybody."

"So, like a paper wealth ... a phantom wealth."

"Yeah, it's paper wealth, you know? For example, currency trading is said to be ten times, 20 times the size of total world trade. Now, world trade employs millions of people, gives jobs to millions of people, and they were dealing in substantial things ... goods, shipping, transportation and things like that. But this 20 times the size of world trade that currency-trading involves— it creates few jobs, does not produce any real new goods and contributes nothing, basically, to the community. And if you take out that 40 percent, the per capita income of the U.S. would be around 20,000, not 36,000."

"You believe that?"

He nods: "That is where it is going to stay. Whatever you may do, the growth would take off from there. It should take off only from 20,000. Unless, of course, you fiddle around with money again."

"Well, we will…" and we both laugh, "but you're suggesting we won't ever be that ballooned again."

"No."

"Right, right … and so it's a systemic collapse."

"Yeah."

"The 40 percent collapse—that's a provocative analysis. Did anybody share that with you, or is that … can we give you the whole credit for it?"

"Well, I've tried to explain this very simple thing to a lot of people, when I say that Malaysia hasn't really recovered. You see, by the same token, if you don't have this fiddling around with money to contribute to the per capita income or GDP of the U.S., then of course your GDP and per capita income would be much lower than it is today."

I shift uncomfortably. Chicken-little prognoses of the world coming to an end ordinarily do not impress. But they do when they come from a capable Cassandra who was far more right than wrong in both his predictions and his actions during the Asian Financial Crisis.

Just recall the arrogance of the International Monetary Fund, which insisted on overnight reforms in return for its billion-dollar bailouts. On paper those demands made economic sense, perhaps. But politically they triggered huge suffering in Asia, from severe unemployment to food shortages. A more nuanced economic reform program could have produced nearly the same benefits without so much suffering. But IMF officials were so sure of themselves that they were largely unyielding. After all, they were dealing with mere 'Asians'—so why listen?

Mahathir not only refused to accept any bailout money, but ignored Western economic orthodoxy. In effect, he temporarily moved the Malaysian economy closer to the more isolated model in Beijing, where the Chinese had long resisted Western exhortations for a more open currency system. Like Chinese leaders, the Malay prime minister was unconvinced that the advice was motivated by altruism. Perhaps countries that were once colonized tend to see the stalking shadows of colonialism almost everywhere when dealing with the West, even on economic issues.

With Western economies in considerable pain just ten years after the Asian Financial Crisis, Mahathir might take some comfort in this. But, in fact, he believes that all will suffer as a result of the "fiddling around with the money". He sighs like the doctor having to inform the patient of pessimistic lab results: "So, we will all suffer, the whole world will be poorer. This is the tragedy."

I say: "Very pessimistic, very pessimistic."

Dr M almost shouts: "It's not pessimism! It's a matter of facing reality. You know, we are in denial now, and those trillions of dollars that are being used to bail out ... that is the wrong strategy. You see, when we bailed out [in the 90s], the world was still intact, the world economy was still intact, and therefore we bail out companies so that they can function in an intact economic environment."

"Right."

"But today, the economic environment has collapsed, and you bail these people out. You're not going to make them do business, because there is less business to be done, unless they are allowed to play again. If they're not allowed to play again—no sub-prime, no nothing—there is nothing to enable them to regain the money which has been given to them."

Me asking: "Bailing a boat out of water that has a huge leak, you mean. Do you look at what's happened with the American economy as primarily an example of just a terrible downturn, or to what extent is it kind of criminal?"

"This crisis is due to abuses of the system. You know, when banks are allowed to lend more than their assets and deposits, they lend more than 30 times, sometimes 50 times. So, they're creating money out of nothing."

"Right."

"They didn't have this money, and yet they were lending, through hedge funds. If you go to borrow 30 times the amount of money you had, they wouldn't lend it to you, but if you put your money in hedge funds, the hedge funds can borrow. So, you now gain the benefit of 30 times the amount of money that you invest."

"And then it blows up in your face—the al-Qaeda financial system. By someone who knows…"

He takes some humor in that. "Yeah."

I push on this point at a later stage of our conversations. Was the pessimism for effect? Or the kind of sober professional analysis one wants from one's leaders?

Me saying: "While we're on this, the disease theory of governance—you've heard this before—but I liked something you said years ago, long before the current American problem, maybe 15, 20 years ago. You said that a deficit in the current account is in effect a kind of attention-deficit disorder, or a self-deception. That's still true today, isn't it?"

"Yeah, they [the Americans] are finding that out."

"Yeah. We're in a lot of debt now."

"Yeah, too much. Now, it's okay to have a deficit. Deficit spending, deficit budgeting is okay. But don't let it grow until it's beyond the point where you cannot repay it. You know, America cannot pay its loans."

"It's a lot of money, isn't it? Are you a pessimist about it?"

"I'm pessimistic about the American management of their finances."

"You have that great phrase I love: 'Stop fiddling with the money'. It's so common sense. Our economists employ all these big terms and big words and you just say, 'They're fiddling with the money.' "

Mahathir smiled at the obvious compliment; he likes

compliments, obviously.

I add: "But your penchant for frankness, for bold statement, for candor. Someone once said that actually, for you, it's a tool of governance, in that you identify with the Malay masses, with their frustrations, their angers, their irritations, their sense of conspiracy; and that it helps you by making comments that maybe people in the West would say are off-the-wall. But it's deliberate; it's not just a moment in which Mahathir flies off the handle, but that it's your way of talking to the masses. It's your way of dialogue. Is there anything to that?"

The doctor nods: "I'm not a loose cannon."

"You're not a loose cannon?"

"I say things because I know I need to say them. Otherwise, people will just try to hide these things, and when you hide things, you'll never cure the person. When you see a person and he has cancer, you don't have to tell him he has cancer, but you must know that he has cancer, and you have to treat it. But if the patient then just says, 'Maybe I'm feeling something else, maybe my doctor is wrong,' then you're trying to cheat yourself, and that's not good."

Dr Mahathir watched the almost embarrassing ordeal of the American health-care debate with great professional interest. So I raise the issue of whether an American president has too little power or too much.

I say: "Obama's being yelled at, screamed at. Maybe there's some racism. His authority is always being questioned. I wonder if you think American presidents could use more time in office." (This question is being posed before the U.S. Congressional elections of November 2010 that left the Obama White House reeling.)

I continue on: "While you had the extraordinary run of 22 years, an American president at his best has eight years—"

"After Roosevelt."

What he means is the American adoption of the 22nd amendment after FDR. It limited U.S. presidents to two terms—eight years. The first critique of that so-called reform came from the first president to whom the limitation first applied. Dwight D. Eisenhower worried that after being re-elected, a second-term president immediately becomes a weak and ineffectual 'lame duck' precisely because everyone knows in a few years he is out of power.

Mahathir shakes his head. "You know, it takes time for any plan or policy to be implemented, and to show results."

I nod.

"If you have only two terms, the first term really is spent trying to learn the job."

"Sure."

"And then you begin to plan…"

"Right."

"And by the end you will be busy trying to win your second term."

"Yeah."

"You cannot concentrate on your plan or policy."

"Right."

"So, when you are re-elected, you have only a short space of time to see to the implementation."

"Right."

"And you need time!" He said that with such emphasis I felt he'd pound the table.

"Yeah, that's what I was thinking. In other words, some presidents have too much time in office ... and some too little."

"Well, yes," he chuckles.

"But you're right. Some don't have enough, you know. I don't mean to be partisan and I don't want to put you in a partisan position, but take for example, Clinton. I think his first term was pretty bad. But the second term, he started to get some things done, despite Monica. And some people felt, boy if he'd had a third term, you know, we might have gotten much more done. So maybe we should amend our Constitution and make it three terms. Twelve years?"

"Yeah, maybe. Three terms, minimum."

"Minimum ... yeah."

"Three terms. Because two terms is not enough, and those [in some other countries] who go for one term as president basically are totally useless. They can't do a thing."

Critics of Asian leaders such as Mahathir will now nod their heads and say, sure, these authoritarian figures always want more time and fewer elections. It figures. They'd never have an election if they could get away with it.

"You know, Dr Mahathir, we Americans often use the term

'soft authoritarian'. This is a term you've heard a million times. The two operative words there for me are 'authority', which I think is a good thing—executive authority, judicial authority, legislative authority ... and the other thing would be 'soft'. But does that term do you any justice at all?"

He shakes his head up and down, seemingly weighing the pros and cons, and adds: "People like to say, 'Well, this man is doing something; he must be a dictator.' But you see, but I wouldn't have lasted if I had been that way. I went through five elections. And [my UMNO political party, of which I was the head] was elected by the people, with good majorities. I went and told the people, 'Look, you give us a two-thirds majority where we form a strong government which can implement things,' and I had my two-thirds majority every time—five times—which means that people understand that when you make a person a leader, you have to give him authority. This idea that you make a person a leader, and after that just start chopping him down, preventing him from exercising any authority at all ... of course he cannot deliver."

I remind Dr M that his 22 years at the pinnacle of power in Malaysia were the equivalent of five and one-half U.S. presidential terms. Even our FDR, who stayed the longest, only had three and a half, which was not quite 13 years in office.

"Do you take the view ... there was a brilliant book written by British journalist Paul Johnson titled *Modern Times*. If you look at all the great human-triggered catastrophes of the 20th century—Stalin, Hitler, Pol Pot, and so forth—it can be read as an argument for gradualism in change. That is, as Aristotle advised, 'beware of extremism'. Beware of the drastic alternatives; beware of the extremes. The best choice and direction is probably somewhere in the middle. Do you think that's right?"

He seems to like this point. "Yeah, that is basically true. But, if you want to accomplish things, and you have a leader who is a dictator, who is authoritarian, but all he does want to do is to help people and develop his country, I think you would want him to be a real leader. But the problem with having a [pure] authoritarian system is that once you have a leader and he goes wrong, there is no way you can remove him."

Me saying: "Well, that's the problem, because then you get into the Hobbesian dilemma. Hobbes, not a great believer in the ability of people to behave themselves, insisted we needed a powerful force to scare the hell out of everybody so they would behave, and then you have true law and order. But what do you do if you don't have a virtuous leader at the top, and you get some jerk, or some evil person … how do you get rid of him? That's the problem, the Hobbesian dilemma. Now, I think you would say, of all the kinds of authoritarianism that are possible (assuming it's not totally incorrect to call you a soft authoritarian) that the kind of system you have is not a bad one, because if you had gone very wrong, at least there would have been a way to get you out of power, right?"

"Yes, in our system, yes. I mean if I had gone wrong, I wouldn't have lasted 22 years. You know, my successor didn't last very long."

He is referring to Abdullah Badawi, who lasted only six years as PM.

I was going to inject that Dr M's own public criticisms didn't help add much to his longevity, but instead I say: "Right … one time, when you were in Los Angeles, you were giving a speech and I was on a table with your then deputy prime minister [Badawi]."

Me continuing: "You know, a very nice man, with a moustache … and I was listening to you. It was clear you were a strong figure, and I was at the same table with him, and I said to myself, 'This guy cannot replace that guy.' [*pause*] Dr M, you should've asked me first!"

We both chortled.

"But you're a tough act to follow. I mean … you're a really tough act to follow."

He says: "You have to be an idealist; otherwise you just want to sit down and do nothing. You have to want to accomplish. But, on the other hand, once you try to do things, you will find that there are so many obstructions which shouldn't be there. I mean why can't people understand that I'm going to do good for you? But that's the reality of life."

I know he's not naïve enough to believe that intellectually, but the way he says it makes me think emotionally he couldn't be more sincere.

"When you stepped down after 22 years, you say you were in a very good position in terms of popularity. But over your 22-year run, several times you considered resignation, but you found the idea unbearable, the idea of resigning and stepping down. So now that you've stepped down, how much agony are you in?"

He shifts his weight in his chair, and looks over my shoulder out past me, then sighs: "There are still lots of things to do. You know, I'm a pragmatic person. I want to do things, to see things done, and to me the greatest reward is to see your dream becoming a reality. It's not the money, it's not the position, it's not the power or whatever. It's achieving your dreams. I mean, not very many people can. So, for me that is most satisfying. So, there are lots of things I would like to do, but I—again, my mother has this influence over me—she always told me, 'Never overstay your welcome. If you go to a friend's house, always remember that he has something else to do. You maybe have nothing to do, and you want to stay and talk to him, but he must have something else to do, so don't overstay,' and I take that to heart. So, even though I feel I could stay on, and even now people say, 'You made a mistake by stepping down,' and all that, I felt that I couldn't. I must not overstay."

"Quit while you're ahead. Quit while you're ahead."

"Yeah, yeah."

A Mahathir Political Point

Serious policy change takes a lot of preparation, good timing and widespread public support. Sometimes only a measure of authoritarianism can foster the centrality of leadership needed to get things done.

You Only Live Twice

Criticizing successors … being ambitious … marathon men of Asia … making people take their medicine

THERE is never enough time to do everything. But success breeds an appetite, sometimes voracious, to get as much done as possible. The great artist never knows when she or he will wake up and have lost the knack, given by God or Allah, of genius. The masterful politician never knows whether cruel fate, objective history or ungrateful public opinion will take back the mandate of authority.

Even writers look back, not always in anger.

Me saying: "It is said of us, as we get on in life and we get older, that we sort of come back to some of the values and enjoyments of when we were youthful. Let's assume there's some truth to this. So what parts of the young, idealistic Mahathir live on today or are resurfacing?"

He is quick to respond: "I feel that I need maybe a thousand years to carry out what I think I need to do. You see, the idealism is still there, but of course I understand the reality of things. Where before I thought that things could be done, now I realize that yes you think it can be done, but it cannot be done, really. See, so I have to accept that, but I still want to do things."

Wanting to do things is not the man in a position of repose—it's the man always in a state of suppose.

Me saying: "Right. Talk a little bit more about ambition, and it arises from your description of your former deputy Anwar Ibrahim as a clever man and very ambitious. Ambition is a good thing, up to a point ... but, here's something that Plato says in his *Republic*, which is his ideal society: you don't want someone to be the Philosopher King who has spent all his life dreaming about becoming the Philosopher King, and thinking about little else. You want someone who could do other, non-governmental things, but accepts the responsibility of ruling because he or she (and Plato would allow a 'she') cares deeply about the 'Republic' and the people in the 'Republic' and (this is the great line) only takes the job for fear of being ruled by a lesser. Great line, that: *fear of being ruled by a lesser.*

"When you were prime minister and you stayed for 22 years and you thought about resigning several times, did you stay on because you feared the country being taken over by a lesser?"

You feel he has thought about this kind of question before: "Well, [the latter] to some extent, yes. But I thought I would put things in place so that the country would go on even by itself; even if we have a bad prime minister, it would still continue. To a certain extent, all the [successes] were there, and you cannot destroy them completely. But even then I worry. What if my successor does something completely wrong? What do I do? Do I keep quiet? And ... this was a worrisome thing for me. Anybody who's responsible, and who believes that he has done something worthwhile, would want to see that thing keep going on."

In truth, Dr Mahathir began knocking down his anointed successor Prime Minister Abdullah Badawi (2003–09) with consistency not long after he himself stepped down. Certainly no one would have accused Dr M of keeping his peace for too long.

Even in the United States, a presidential successor is traditionally handled by his predecessor with kid gloves. In recent times Bill Clinton had nary a negative word about President George W. Bush, who has said almost nothing so far about President Obama.

But for Dr M, it seemed, Badawi was bad medicine for Malaysia right from the start, even though his quiet-speaking, scholarly-appearing successor had come from UMNO and had been his chosen man all along. Logically, under those circumstances, how bad could Badawi have been?

Even if Badawi was as miscast as Mahathir would often suggest, saying so publicly made his besieged successor seem even more hapless than he probably was. The spectacle was particularly odd, because the chances of Mahathir getting his old job back were zero, and Dr M surely knew it.

And so perhaps it was probably the role of public educator, more than incumbent office holder, that Mahathir most wanted to take with him? Let's try that idea out.

"But people say, 'Ah, this guy Mahathir. He is out of office and he can't shut up' … and they are always putting his views in the papers and he's criticizing everyone and so forth. I guess what I'm saying is that it's really hard to let go, isn't it?"

He sighs and shuffles in his chair as if he might want to hide under the desk, then says: "It is hard to let go. When you have a plan for something and you have to let go and let somebody else get in, and you don't know what he's going to do, it's very difficult."

Badawi held the top spot for only half a dozen years, in a region famous for its long-distance political thoroughbreds. President Suharto, the old general who never seemed to die but in the end just faded away, the once-apolitical military man who engineered the coup against Sukarno that liquidated a lot of communists (as well as many Chinese Indonesians who weren't communists)—he stayed atop Indonesia for 32 years. Lee Kuan Yew of Singapore held the PM job for 31 years. Love them or hate them, these tough marathon men were something else.

To be sure, Dr M held on but two decades plus, and that is something special for the circumstances. Malaysia, for all its governance faults, has been far more of a practicing democracy than Indonesia, and its politics have been more election-driven and coalition-driven than Singapore's.

But for my part, just thinking about running a place as complex as Singapore, Malaysia or Indonesia is daunting and exhausting. So I ask him whether the stress of those 22 years ever reached the point where he thought of resorting to medicines to ease things.

Dr M shakes his head vigorously, denying letting stress get to him, saying that as a good doctor, he takes his own medical advice—he exercises virtually daily.

"So, you were not really aware of feeling stressed. Is that true?"

"Well, people say that when you are stressed it will show on your face. Well, people say that I don't look my age."

"You do not look 84, that's for sure."

"Yeah."

"And you certainly don't talk like you're 84. And to ride horses, as you do, you have to be in pretty good physical shape, don't you?"

"Well, yes."

"'Cause I know when I ride horses I can't move for the next two days!"

"No," he chuckles, "I do some physical exercise. I do treadmill, and then lift some weights."

"Every day? Or a few times a week?"

"Practically every day."

"It's boring, isn't it?"

"Boring?"

"Yeah, to do exercise, isn't it?"

"I know, but you also know you have to do it. I'm a doctor, you know!"

We both laugh.

I add: "That reminds me about a great line about you, by the way. This may not be fair, but one of your critics has pointed out that, like a good doctor, Dr M pushes things down your throat. Did you bridle at that?"

His face brightens up like a kid offered a lollipop: "No, I think it's half true!"

"It is half true?"

"You want to give medicine but it's no good if the person doesn't take it. So, you have to see to it that he takes it."

He reminds me of some of the family doctors I have known, but few had Mahathir's sense of humor. I say: "Medicine that is taken generally works better than medicine that isn't."

We both laugh. But he is serious.

He says: "That's true. It's a simple dictum."

In a manner of speaking, the best doctors are almost always soft authoritarians. They make you take the medicine that's good for you, whether you like it or not.

A Mahathir Political Point

A developing nation must always take its meds, whether the patients (its people) want to or not.

The Anti-Semitism Controversy Never Dies

Muslim-Jewish angst ... no need to change views ... Jews protect themselves ... we are where they were

Author's note: Dr Mahathir never asked to review his direct quotes, much less review the actual manuscript. But his controversial views on Israel, Israelis and the Jews are sometimes all that Westerners know about him. Thus, to avoid misunderstanding, I sent this chapter to Malaysia for him to offer his comments and corrections. He had none.

MAHATHIR is a troubling paradox. You have figured out by now that it is my instinct that he is almost precisely the kind of cosmopolitan Muslim leader the West has been searching for. We need to locate and engage not neo-collaborationists whom anyone can see through but true Muslim leaders who have immense credibility with their own people, yet who stand for peace and cooperation. For many years, that man—however idiosyncratic—was Mahathir Mohamad of Malaysia.

And yet his image with some Western and Jewish leaders is just this side of notorious. It turns out that Dr M became known in many circles in the West mainly as an anti-Semite. Or merely as an anti-Semite. Or even only as an anti-Semite. This becomes a sad tale indeed.

And yet for many years he was a Muslim leader of a mainly Muslim nation well equipped to provide exceptional adult operational perspective on the so-called 'clash of civilizations' between the religious Islamic world and the secular Western world.

There are tragedies to life, and then there are tragedies to life— but this was a big one.

Please consider that Mahathir offers almost everything you could want in a 'moderate' (but he doesn't like this adjective) or mainstream (this, he feels, is slightly better) Muslim leader.

He was a mainstream/moderate Muslim with an internationalist outlook. He was a practicing Muslim who fought to isolate his religious crazies more skillfully (and relatively humanely) than any contemporary politician did or could. And he had—and has—an honest respect for all religions, including Judaism and Christianity.

He genuinely believed, almost Gandhi-like, in the absolute necessity of nonviolence. He was even passionate in advocating that all nations agree to limit their annual expenditures on armaments to one percent of their national wealth. The depth of his military pacifism perhaps is deep. It has philosophical depth.

But many Jewish critics in the West saw him as nothing more than an arrogant and dangerous anti-Semitic witchdoctor who, had he the power to do so, would threaten Israel's very existence.

Truth and perspective were lost in the continuing storm.

Dr M was kept under the anti-Semite spotlight by a number of factors. One was the misleadingly selective methodology of the U.S. news media in reporting only 'newsworthy' aspects of what he said and did. Once the Western media had concluded he was a rank anti-Semite, it chose to report mainly comments and developments about him that confirmed this image as an anti-Semite. In other words, if what he said was what he had said before, then that was 'news'—get it? (I don't and never have.)

Another factor was the excessive willingness of many in the West to assume the worst about someone they knew relatively little, and to accept too readily analogies to Hitler and the Holocaust as if those extremely tragic events could almost be an every-other-day occurrence.

But—and this is important—Dr M himself made matters more difficult by speaking in a bravado manner that, in effect, conflated verbal brashness with intellectual integrity. He expanded the right to say whatever he wanted into actually spewing forth whatever he wanted, whenever he wanted to say it notwithstanding the possible, even predictable, misinterpretation or misunderstanding. Even while knowing that the Western media was viewing him from its determined lens, he had no reservations about providing more ammunition to his critics.

This is all a tragedy. Dr Mahathir's anti-Semitism is *illusion*, not reality. He does not think of himself as one and, after hours of conversation, your author—a former New Yorker, married to a

Jew, with a daughter who is thus Jewish, and with past decades as a resident of New York, the so-called 'Jewish capital of the world'— is pretty certain that Dr M is not one.

Let's look at the record.

Offending public statements by Dr Mathathir, when he was in office, were invariably intended by him—he says—to rally his mainly Muslim audience into consensus and understanding. Whether that tactic was effective or not is hard to pin down. But toward the end of his reign in Malaysia, his stature across the Islamic world had risen to a very high level. His famous 2003 speech to an Islamic leaders assembly in Kuala Lumpur, selectively quoted in the Western media as an anti-Semitic diatribe, was viewed in the Islamic world as a capstone to his career. (Read "He's Much Harder On His Muslims Than Those Jews" in the Appendix on pages 233–243 and you can decide for yourself what his goal was.)

Presumably if he had repeatedly declared solidarity with the Israeli government's policies and practices on Palestine and other controversial issues, a good part of his base would have figured him for a CIA front. For that issue he had tried to position himself just as Richard Nixon (as U.S. president) had with the China issue.

Usually—in his most goading speeches—the goal was to show that the recent downturn in their fortunes was the consequence of events beyond their control (such as the near-disastrous Asian Financial Crisis). Or it was to show that their misfortunes were the consequence of their historic unwillingness to outwork their competitors.

Dr Mahathir never gave a speech that had a title or an aim like *Now Let Me Attack and Let Us Together Destroy Jews and Israel*. On the contrary, his aim was to berate the Islamic world for falling so far behind modernity. He was the CEO at the company retreat exhorting his employees to outdo the 'other guys'. He was, if you will, the fiery coach of the football team at halftime exhorting his players. What's more, like a football coach preparing his team to play the cross-town rival, it made no sense politically to say anything nice about Israel and the Jews whose awesome success Dr M viewed as a continuing rebuke of his fellow Muslims.

But too often, he went too far. For the head of a major government knows full well that his every sentence, word and, indeed, gesture go under the global mass-communication microscope. So what is said to make one kind of point in Kuala Lumpur is read in another way in Tel Aviv, or indeed in New York.

The Western media will always help to stir hysteria on this kind of issue. By the time any given Mahathirism had bounced around the world several times—in and out of 30-second TV news reports and into a 900-word newspaper column and, not to mention countless blogs of varying qualities—it has attained a vibrant, if destructive, life of its own. Consider these Mahathirisms:

- "Of late because of their power and their apparent success they have become arrogant. And arrogant people, like angry people, will make mistakes, will forget to think." (1997)

- "When a person of Jewish origin does this kind of thing [commits an international financial crime], the effect is the same as when a Muslim carried out something akin to terrorism." (1997)

- "We do not want to say that this is a plot by the Jews, but in reality it is a Jew who triggered the currency plunge, and coincidentally Soros is a Jew. It is also a coincidence that Malaysians are mostly Moslem. Indeed, the Jews are not happy to see Moslems progress. If it were Palestine, the Jews would rob Palestinians. Thus this is what they are [right now] doing to our country." (1997)

- "Japanese newspapers put down my talk to me being anti-Semitic ... but they pick up one sentence in which I said the Jews control the world. Well, the reaction of the world shows that they control the world." (2003)

- "Israel is a small country. There are not many Jews in the world. But they are so arrogant they defy the whole world." (2003)

- "But today the Jews rule this world by proxy. They get others to fight and die for them." (2003)

To many Western ears, blunt statements like these are hurtfully insensitive. They certainly do not seem good-willed, even if intended to develop a general theme (why are Muslims in general so far behind Jews?) that is less anti-Semitic than indirectly complimentary.

So, to get the record straight, I ask Dr M to give it to us straight. The tense Muslim-Jewish issue, after all, is at the front line of the East-West battlefield.

He starts by explaining, with some annoyance, that there seems to be a penalty assessed for even having an opinion on any issue that diverges from that of the current Israeli government. Of course, almost all of his comments are at odds with Israeli policy, of almost any Israeli government—and therefore with American policy.

I say: "I hope you don't get irritated with me for raising this, but have there been any comments you've ever made on Zionism that you'd like to take back?"

It's a long shot to play. Public figures rarely like to admit a mistake. Mahathir is a proud man. Besides, any modification, however brave, might be viewed in some Islamic circles as a cowardly retreat.

But if he does want to 'contextualize' the issue in a more nuanced way, what would be a better place than a book—or a better time than now?

He doesn't take too long to answer: "No, I have said them because I believe what I said was correct."

I try it one more time: "But if I go back over say, all of your statements over the years on Zionism, you're okay with all of them?"

"Yes, I'm okay." No big pause.

I frown: "Well, I have to tell you as a columnist, occasionally I'd write something and ten hours later I wish I could pull it back … it wasn't perfect, it wasn't quite right. But you're comfortable with everything you said."

"Yeah."

"Alright." Sigh, disappointment. Frankly, I was hoping for some headline-making backtracking!

Sensing my disappointment, he shifts his weight a little.

"When I said that the Zionists control the world through proxy—the U.S. is its proxy—I meant it. I told the whole world that the Jews rule the world by proxy … my God, there was such a row! 'This anti-Semitic person said that…' but it's true!"

It cannot be that he actually believes the world is ruled by Jews, whether via go-betweens or otherwise. Surely what he means is that their influence is extensive, which it is; and that U.S. support vastly increases Israeli clout in international affairs. (If I were an Israeli, I'd certainly want to engineer extensive global influence for my country!)

His penchant for hyperbole is a mirror of his penchant for Petronas overstatement. Representing a country with a population smaller than even Afghanistan or Iraq—but 44th or so on the list of nations—Dr Mahathir believes talking softly in this world will get you nowhere, especially when you don't really possess a single big stick.

So I figure why hold back, and ask: "Are you anti-Semitic?"

The directness caught him a little off balance: "Huh?"

"Are you anti-Semitic?"

"I'm not. I'm not. I have a lot of Jewish friends, very close friends."

Well, Hitler didn't, so I guess that's a start. "And you're not anti-Jew?"

"I'm not anti-Jew, why should I be? But for what they [the Israeli government in Gaza and so on] are doing, I'm against that. Anymore than I can say I'm anti-American. I'm not anti-American, but when you do wrong things, I'm entitled to criticize as much as you are entitled to criticize the wrong things that I do."

It's clear where he is going with this, so I might as well say it: "But sometimes in America, being critical of Israeli policies is conflated with anti-Semitism and anti-Jew, right?"

On this he quickly agrees, but then takes it in a different direction: "Somebody wrote about this 'Holocaust Industry'. It has become an industry. You know, you put memorials here about the Holocaust and all that, and you cannot even reduce the estimated figure of six million dead by one person ... that's anti-Semitic."

He has a very minor point but it trivializes the issue for me. It's far too cynical a way to categorize the desire to deal with feeling and memory. All holocausts—whether Jewish, Armenian, Kosovo or Cambodian—deserve proper and permanent memorial. We must always remember the worst we have done in order to hope to achieve the best we can do, in part by avoiding the evil in ourselves.

And is any memorial or humanitarian effort ever blemish free? Of course not!

That some overly entrepreneurial Cambodian hucksters rake in a few extra riel by capitalizing on grief hardly invalidates the deserved respect for the enormity of the Cambodian holocaust. At the same time, do I believe some of my Jewish friends are too quick to take offense and too slow to forgive? Yes I do.

But back to our Dr M. He is such a giant of Asia, in many respects, and yet he piddles around with a handful of relatively cheap points.

So I try some more: "I just want to read you a few things. I had my researcher pull this up. In *The Malay Dilemma*, which everyone agreed was a deeply provocative, important, ground-breaking book for its time, your first book, in 1970, you wrote this: 'The Jews, for example, are not merely hook-nosed, but understand money instinctively.' You want to still stay with that?"

Dr M shrugs. He's not for backing down. Among other things, he calculates that any rhetorical retreat, even if viewed in the West as statesmanlike, will be widely viewed by Muslim Malays as pure face-losing kowtow to Jewish pressure. He'd rather take heat from the West than lose credibility by seeming to try to play both sides of the fence.

It's just that such insulting stereotypes tend only to fit some of the facts. Some of my best Asian students in California cannot do math. Some of the sweetest, least-angry people I have known are Korean. All Germans aren't Nazis deep in their souls. Not all Dutch people are cheap ('Dutch treat'?). Every Malaysian I have done business with is honest and un-devious. None of my Japanese friends are warmongers.

And many close friends of mine are Jewish. A few of them do display special prowess with finances, but only a few. Many are academics who can barely balance their check books. My wife leaves the family finances to me to figure out, even though I'm not Jewish—and she is.

Some famous financial brainiacs are Jewish and some are not. Siegmund Warburg was. John Reed and Walter Wriston of Citibank were not. Perhaps the most famous of all financial types—all-time—was J.P. Morgan … not a Jew.

On the other hand—more contemporarily—President Barack Obama's Secretary of the Treasury, Timothy Geithner, is Jewish; legendary former Chairman of the Federal Reserve Paul Volcker is Jewish; and Ben Bernanke, Chairman of the United States Federal Reserve, is Jewish. (You know, so what? They don't all meet in the same temple and try to figure out how to mess up Islamic economies!)

On another other hand, their boss Barack Obama is not Jewish; his Secretary of State Hillary Clinton is not Jewish; Secretary of Defense Robert Gates is not; CIA Director Leon Panetta is not; Senate Majority Leader Harry Reid is not; and House Minority Leader Nancy Pelosi is not. What's more, on the U.S. Supreme

Court—the powerful judicial branch of government—only two of the court's nine members are Jewish, which means they are seriously outnumbered ... though there are no Muslims, unfortunately.

Conclusion: like Malaysia, the U.S. is a polyglot country with many competing ethnicities, religions and creeds. A Jewish cabal at the top it is not.

So does Dr M want to revise his views about the Jews?

No, Dr M wants to hold firm that Jews more or less run the Western world, because they know how to play with the money better than any other group (however 'group' is defined).

Him saying: "Yes, yes. There are people who are very smart in this thing. It's really a compliment. I don't understand the fear ... I mean you know that the banks in America, you look at the Fed in America ... who runs them? Why cannot we see what is a fact? I say things that are factual. You can say that I'm wrong; you can, but prove that I'm wrong. But when I say something that is factual about other people, nobody accuses me of being anti-other people, but if you say anything at all against the Jews, you are immediately anti-Semitic. Why? I mean you call Muslims ... all Muslims are terrorists, their Prophet is a terrorist, et cetera."

I don't personally know a single American who'd claim that all Muslims are terrorists, but surely there are many such ignorant Americans in the U.S. (some Americans actually believe President Obama is a Muslim). So Dr M is right about that. At the same time, statements are either true—such as, U.S. foreign policy is totally under the influence of the Israel lobby—or they are false.

I had to tell him how I felt: "I would say that any American who says that all Muslims are terrorists is an idiot as well as a bigot, or at least tragically misinformed. Now, you used the language, 'Jews are not merely hook-nosed'. I mean, did you have to say that? I mean, Obama has big ears, and I have a red nose, and … who cares?"

It can sound as if there might be a whole class or ethnicity of people he doesn't like the look of.

Sometimes Dr M plays the dumb possum, not often, just every once in a while: "Well, I said that. I can't deny that I said that in my book. I mean, people can confirm this."

"I know, I'm not asking you to deny that you wrote it or said it. What I am wondering is, if you re-wrote the book today though, would you leave the 'hook-nosed' in or take it out?"

The stubborn Mahathir shakes his head: "Well, Arabs are also hook-nosed. They are also Semitic people. See, why are they so sensitive about it? I have a reputation for having a big nose in Malaysia. They draw a cartoon of me with a big nose. I thought it was a joke."

I guess he's saying he'd leave it in—some joke. So I try to make the point that "Well, six million of those hook-nosed people died in the Second World War…"

This is his response: "Yeah, we can't even say 5,999,999."

I simply ignore that and try a semi-flip answer by noting that at least no one is trying to push the number in the other direction and make it seven million.

Okay, another try: "In 2003 you told an assembly of leaders

of 57 nations that Jews 'rule the world by proxy, and get others to fight and die for them'. Then you said, you called for a 'final victory by the world's 1.3 billion Muslims, who cannot be defeated by a few million Jews'."

He looks right at me: "Well, in terms of numbers. If they [Muslims] behave like Jews, they cannot be defeated."

"Right, but the Nazis used the term 'final solution' and you use the term 'final victory'. Do you want to destroy all of the Jews?"

His voice lifts a little here, a slight touch of healthy anger surfaces: "No, it's not a question of destroying all the Jews. I mean, if you defeat people, it doesn't mean that you destroy them. You see, you defeated Japan; look at what Japan is now. You look at Germany, which was also defeated, but at times they are much stronger than most of the victors."

"Right. So, when you say 'final victory over the—"

"I don't mean what Hitler meant. I'm not going to throw them into gas chambers, you know? But, we … I mean, it is shameful that 1.3 billion Muslims cannot handle a few million Jews."

This is his central point: not that he so much resents Jewish accomplishments but that he greatly regrets relative Islamic backwardness. He would wish the Islamic world united enough to demand changes in U.S. policy toward the Middle East, for example. He's frustrated that UN Security Council demands for Israeli observance of past resolutions meets a U.S. veto every time.

Note that in Dr M's mind the Malay and the Muslim problem overlap.

Me asking: "You wrote a terrific book that centered on the Malay dilemma. Is the Malay dilemma [in fact] a Muslim dilemma?"

He thinks for a few ticks, then admits: "A little bit, it is."

"Is the Malay dilemma easing as an impediment to the country's progress?"

"We have overcome quite a lot of things which stood in the way, but there's still a lot to do."

"So, your view is that when you say things about how the Jews are running everything, which is such obvious hyperbole it's hard to imagine serious people taking you seriously, it's less a commentary on the Jews than on your own people?"

He nods: "It's about the Muslims. I told them, learn from the Jews. I said they were oppressed for 2,000 years, and yet they have been able to succeed. In other parts of my speech, if you read the whole speech, you will know that in a way I was complimenting the Jews, but they pick on that particular word, and they claim that I'm anti-Semitic, of course."

"Which you deny that you are…"

"I'm not." He points to the fact that even today he helps fund a small two-way exchange program for students from Malaysia and Israel.

"Your rival in Singapore, Lee Kuan Yew, has used this line: 'I am not as smart as an Israeli.' That's kind of what you mean, though. Right?"

"Yeah, same thing. One has to admit that the Jews have got tremendous capability. They have super brains."

Dr Mahathir doesn't realize it but Jews and Israelis would happily forgo the attempt at a mass compliment if Muslim leaders would accept them more as individuals than some sort of superhuman model minority.

At the same time, Mahathir's assessment of Israelis as a nation of super brains is a common view in Asia. What else can account for its seemingly disproportionate success on the world stage? The thin borderline between admiration and stereotyping is too thin to always definitively delineate reality.

I plow on: "Why do you think that is true of the Israelis?"

"I think it's being oppressed over 2,000 years. They have to defend themselves. They're forced into ghettos where they have to think about how to survive. See, people who are oppressed either disappear, or they develop strategies to preserve themselves."

"So, you're thinking it's largely environmental."

"Yeah, it's largely environmental."

"But do you see any genetic basis to it?"

"Well, if it is genetic I think the Arabs should have the same character. They went through a very prolonged experience, and they survived, and obviously they have learned something about survival, and they are where they are because they have survived."

I go on to the next Tour Stop in the 'Mahathir on the Jews' Show.

I say: "You once said that you had definite information that financier George Soros, who you identified as a Jew, was responsible for Malaysia's currency problems back in the late 90s. In fact, most economic historians would back some version of that assertion.

"You stated, 'We do not want to say that this is a plot by the Jews, but in reality it was a Jew who triggered the currency plunge, and coincidentally Soros is a Jew. It is also a coincidence that Malaysians are mostly Muslim. Indeed, the Jews are not happy to see Muslims progress. In Palestine, the Jews rob Palestinians. Thus, this is what they are doing to our country.'

"So, you do see the Jews as conspiring to keep you down?"

He nods quietly.

Me continuing: "The Jews, as you say, because of their survivalistic—indeed, their extreme survivalistic edge—protect their interests aggressively."

He nods: "They seem to come together."

"But do you think they would like to see the Muslim world kept down?"

He nods: "Because they see the Muslim world as producing terrorists, and thus attacking them. That's how they see it."

Me adding: "But actually, if the 'Muslim world' were to begin—that's like a huge term, that's like saying 'Asia'—but if the 'Muslim world' were to begin to regain its former glory in terms of wealth, and prominence, and science, and math, and learning … it might reduce Muslim terrorism."

Dr M is obviously happy to move into this direction: "Well, that was what happened before. You know, during that period [the 15th century under Ferdinand and Isabella], when the Europeans were carrying out pogroms against the Jews, where did they run to, before the United States? They all went to Muslim countries. That is why in Algeria, in Morocco, there are lots of Jews. When the Christians re-conquered Spain, the Muslims and the Jews were given three choices. Either you convert to Christianity, or you migrate to North Africa, or you will be executed. That's the choice.

"But, when the Muslims were ruling Spain, the Jews thrived. They were doing well; in fact, they were among the advisors to the Muslim rulers of Spain. Their relationship with the Arabs was very good. They spoke Arabic; they have Arabic names. Lots of Jews adopt Muslim names, and they speak Arabic, and they live in Muslim countries. Whenever they are in trouble in Europe, they invariably go to Muslim countries, that is, until the United States was founded. Then, of course, they migrated to the United States."

"Right…"

"This is historically true."

Clearly, he is proud of this history, a relatively rare chunk of Islamic history of which he feels he can indeed be proud: "Then you said—and we're almost done with this—'I did not say there was a Jewish conspiracy, that was one of the options. We did not accuse the Jews of causing the currency plunge, but it looked like they triggered the currency prices. Are we not allowed to say anything about it? We feel as though we are not allowed to say anything irritating concerning other countries.' "

I have to laugh: "That sure sounds like you!"

So does this, another Mahathirism I throw at him: 'When a person of Jewish origin does this kind of thing—currency intervention—the effect is the same as when a Muslim carried out something akin to terrorism."

He takes this all in carefully, then says a little slowly: "I just want to give my view. I've been called anti-Semitic, but I believe that if anybody does wrong, I have a right to criticize. You can criticize everybody else. You can call the Muslims terrorists, say the Prophet is the leader of terrorists, and all that, and nobody calls you any particular name. But you can't even say simple things; you can't even state the truth about the Jews, without being called anti-Semitic. Now, labeling, of course, is the best way of killing a person, the political career of any person. He's labeled, therefore he is anti-Semitic, so of course, what he says is not to be taken seriously, to be accepted, because of his being anti-Semitic. I once said, the Jews rule the world by proxy."

"Yes, you once did say that."

"I said that, yes, and there is a reason for that. Because America will always defend Israel, no matter what it does, which is wrong, and the Jewish lobby in America is very powerful. That is something that is a fact. Everybody knows this, though not everybody will say it. And their influence over America is overwhelming. And their effect on America also is overwhelming. The present world financial crisis, if you care to look at the names of all the banks, the people who run these banks, they are Jewish people."

Here we go again with Jews and money!!

He continues: "Well, people say we should call them Americans, and not Jews. But, if you call them Americans, you are blaming a lot of other people who are quite innocent. This playing around with money to make more money, and thus to undermine the whole financial system is basically Goldman Sachs, Morgan Stanley and all the rest. If they are only Americans, it's alright, but they are also very close to Israel."

He continues: "So that if you say anything against Israel, you become anti-Semitic. But prove to me that it is not true that the main players in the present financial crisis aren't of Jewish origin. They are the people who invented the banks, who invented a lot of things financial. They are the ones who play with the money, mostly. So, why can't you say that, by and large, this crisis is due to the Jewish attempt to make more money for themselves?"

I ignore that because it is such a broad assertion as to defy reasoned refutation. Yes, people want to make money; the financial market is a good place to make money; some people who want to make lots of money are Jewish. So where does that take us? But pushing it further by suggesting that *all* Jews *only* want to make money, and at the expense of Muslims, strikes many as stereotyping—and weak analysis. It's like suggesting that ... well ... all Muslims are terrorists. In fact, some Jews are poor; others are professional orchestra players who don't make a great deal of money; many are grade-school teachers who are anything but financially motivated; some run the Fed. *Please!!*

Okay, so I have had my say, too.

Now, let's try for some balance. Where Mahathir's critics are unfair is their penchant for isolating his 'Jewish' assertions from the context in which they appeared.

Me saying to Dr M: "My Lu, the senior researcher on this book, a distinguished degree holder from the blue-chip Fletcher School of Law and Diplomacy, told me, regarding the 'six or seven of his more notorious statements', in all cases the Western media took out those sentences and isolated them from their contexts. She found—and I agree—that the statements were contained in the context not of being anti-Semitic but saying, 'If a mere eight million Jews can achieve all of this, why the heck can't us Malays or Muslims do better?' So you use this stuff as a goad, as a prod, as an incentive, as a motive … is that right?"

"Yeah, in the same speech I blamed the Muslims, because they are not patient, they are not persistent, not consistent."

"Not consistent?"

"Yeah. They are not united. You know, the number of Jews in America is very, very small. The number of Jews in the world is very small, but they act together, and because of that, they are effective. It took them a long time … 2,000 years of pogroms, and you know, the Holocaust, et cetera, for them to realize that they have to come together and protect their interests."

My own view is that the cohesiveness of the world Jewish community is vastly overrated. In many respects Jews can be as internally quarrelsome as any so-called 'community' (a much over-used word in public discourse). Perhaps my growing up on

Long Island, with many Jewish playmates, and living for decades in Manhattan, with many Jewish colleagues, brought me close to the true noisy, feisty, self-analytical and self-critical nature of the Jewish 'community'.

I decide not to pursue this but instead say: "So, you don't really blame them for behaving the way they do."

"Well, they have to protect themselves."

I say: "You're just pointing out what they do."

"Today the Muslims are in the same position as the Jews used to be. So why don't you [Muslims] be patient? Why don't you plan, strategize, and acquire the right knowledge and the right instruments, strategies, and all that in order to protect yourself?"

Me again: "Just to nail this down. So you're saying Muslims are in the same place today as the Jews used to be?"

He nods.

I ask him whether playing the blame game really does anybody any good.

He nods again, quite agreeably, adding: "You know, when the financial crisis hit Indonesia in 1997, the Indonesians blamed the Chinese."

"Right."

"They killed the Chinese. They rioted. They burned up the shops of the Chinese."

"Right."

"Simply because the Chinese, although they are also Indonesian, still retained their identification with China."

I say to him this example should tell us something. For when you search for people to blame, pointing fingers at any one group and suggesting they are the cause of your troubles, a lot of innocent people can get hurt. Do anti-Semitic statements by Dr M, however intended to rally the troops, encourage actual anti-Semitic feeling in the Islamic world?

Dr M looks at me with those large round eyes, reflecting quietly. He says nothing.

It's time to move on to another subject. We've done as much with this one as we can. Perhaps some day his critics in the West will come to see his verbal antics as little more than the politician playing his own political games. Much like the American politician blaming our current economic woes on the Chinese (or in the 90s, the Japanese), when he or she knows better, Dr M can play the blame game with the best of them.

The West's over-reaction doesn't bother him much. It only burnishes his standing with certain sectors of his constituency. They feel almost no one stands up to Israel. But they think Dr M does—and always has.

No matter. Mahathir is out of power now.

But when he was in power, at the top of his game, he was anything but the kind of Muslim political figure the West has come to fear since 9/11. He was smarter than almost every other Muslim ruler, and if he was an anti-Semite at all, in his mind he was an anti-Israeli—so outspoken, in fact, that who would have been more qualified to broker an Arab-Israeli peace?

If that thought ever entered his mind—and he dismisses it with a wave of his hand—we in the West missed that. What we may also have missed is a bridge-builder clever enough to help bring us all together. Asking a flawed but talented man to be perfect is to sacrifice the good on the altar of the ideal.

As the special section in the Appendix on his 2003 speech to Islamic leaders shows, in his heart Dr M does not resent Israel's enormous achievement but he deplores Islamic insipidness. The more Islam stumbles, and the higher Israel climbs, the more his figurative blood pressure boils.

Perhaps this is another reason why, even in his mid-eighties, he exercises so much.

The World is Not Enough

Afghanistan tragedy ... non-universality of democracy ... China coming apart? ... fears for America

AT that World Economic Forum convention in New York in 2002 just months after the successful Islamic terrorist attack on the World Trade Center towers, Dr Mahathir made points that stand up well in the light of a decade later.

He expressed, perhaps surprisingly, sympathy for President George W. Bush's almost immediate lunge of the knife into Muslim Afghanistan. Any American president would have had to react forcefully, he told me. But he also said that deliberately waiting, rather than immediately reacting, sometimes added sympathy for your position. Showing restraint and appearing uneager to respond with an eye for an eye can spotlight the terrorists as the true barbarians they are—and render you the true and preferred cosmopolitan humanitarian.

Dr Mahathir frequently preaches that line to Muslim audiences as well, as vividly evident in his shrewd Islamic Summit Conference address in 2003. But he understood the shock of 09/11 on the American people and the pressure on its president not to look lame.

Where he hoped the Bush administration would not go wrong was in Iraq.

Don't go there, was his advice; avoid invading another Muslim country. "Keep it up," he said to me, "and you may wind up with whole large swaths of the world where Americans will not be welcomed." He viewed the mind of the Bush administration as at best a blunt instrument.

It was against this background that we waded into the American condition today.

Me saying: "As you know, the new American Obama government has dropped the term 'War on Terror', to which I think you would probably say good riddance. But we're still screwing around in Afghanistan. We're still stuck in Iraq. I remember talking to you— you probably don't remember, but I remember talking to you about it in early 2002—and you said, 'Afghanistan ... probably Bush has to, but don't go into Iraq,' you know? And we didn't listen. We should've listened. I listened, but I'm not important. Now, we have a new President Obama, and we're in Afghanistan [almost 10 years later!]. How concerned are you that this could be the swamp that sucks in an otherwise good president?"

"Well, frankly, I don't like the way the Afghans run their country, but to have a country like the U.S., this big power going around correcting everybody and everything..."

Dr M shakes his head in frustration. Hoping (not to mention fighting) for better governance in Afghanistan, he continues, is a fool's errand: "Over time, the U.S. may get rid of these [undesirable] things, but you can't go and correct them overnight any more than you can change the Afghan mindset. They are used to tribalism, they are used to war, and they are used to their warlords. That's their system. And of course it's the Americans, especially, who say, 'But if they are democratic, everything is solved.' It's not. You create a lot of problems for countries who try to practice democracy when their people do not understand democracy."

As an American, I am not supposed to believe this apostasy. But as a journalist who travels around the world, it is hard to believe Dr M is wrong.

"You've been saying one-size-doesn't-fit-all for a long time." Democracy can hardly be an all-purpose answer, if, in many political situations, it has created so many problems.

"You see what happened to Bangladesh: one government is elected, it goes up, the people have demonstrations, they go on strike, they bring the government down, the other government goes up, and the same thing happens. Practically, there is no government."

A much milder but still illustrative example of bumbling democracy occurs in Japan. There, a PM comes and goes sometimes in a matter of months, as the economy stagnates and the polity marinates in the poison of a parliamentary system that produces almost nothing.

I add: "And of course, across Asia and beyond, some of the most successful systems of governance have been not particularly democratic."

Nodding his head in agreement, Mahathir then refers to Iraq, the other recent military invasion by the United States of which he doubts Machiavelli would not have approved: "Nope. If you take a headcount of all the people who have died during Saddam's time, compared to what has happened now—since he has been gone— one would think that maybe we need Saddam to come back."

It's a wicked thought, to be sure. Few people around the world shed a tear when the Saddam Hussein regime was deposed by the U.S. invasion. Then again, trying to export democracy by invasion is a fool's errand.

I agree: "If you did a cost-benefit analysis, you mean, the least-worst situation might have been Saddam. But, you see, we're Americans and so we know everything."

We both laugh.

He says: "Of course. I never denied that. That's one thing I believe as much as you believe in the Bible!"

He was betting that this American journalist was a typical Western materialist atheist. But the truth is, I've been working with my Jesuit friends at Loyola Marymount University, where I teach, to try to rekindle my Catholicism, however tamped down the embers of decades of neglect.

Me asking: "All of us who've been through Vietnam, whether as observers or participants, say of Afghanistan, 'Isn't this another Vietnam?' So you're President Obama, what would *you* do? What do we do?"

The answer comes back at me with almost surprising force:

"Pull out. Pull out. The timing is something else that can be decided, but you must pull out. You see, the U.S. has never won a war, except in Grenada."

It's almost as if he actually doesn't want the U.S. to seriously mess up—an unexpected concern if he's truly so hardcore anti-American.

Then I snap to: "Except in *where?*"

"Grenada!"

"Oh, right! How could I ever have forgotten?"

It was in 1983 that President Ronald Reagan ordered the U.S. invasion of the minuscule, lightly populated, allegedly going-communist island nation in the Caribbean. The resistance consisted of well-trained Cuban special forces, but not in great numbers. Admirers of the operation depict it as a great victory. My own view is that, in the annals of wars that you cannot really lose, this one might make it to the top of the list. You know what? Cheers to the late Reagan for that!

He continues: "All the rest—you lost in North Korea, when you were fighting against the Chinese. You have to accept that there is a North Korea, which is communist. You lost in Vietnam, you lost Somalia … and you have not won in Afghanistan. You see, you should learn the lesson that today's war is not like yesterday's war."

"It's not like World War Two."

"No, no. Before, you fight in a war, you win a war, and you sign a treaty, and the war is over. Today, you can fight, and win, and defeat your enemies, sign the treaty, but the people will not accept it."

"Mhm."

"They will take pot shots on you," he says, especially referring to Afghanistan. "They will kill your people…"

"Basically, forever."

"Yeah, forever! Until they get back their freedom." He means freedom from us … as the occupying power, however excellent our true intent may arguably be.

"Right."

"You see, this is something that the U.S. has not realized. All these big weapons that you are making, can you use them? You can't."

"Right, right. When I was last in Vietnam, talking up some people in Hanoi, and I said, 'You know, it's still the view of some in the Pentagon that had we just stayed there longer and done more, then we would have won,' and I said, 'What do you think of that?', and they shook their heads. And then they said, 'You know, what you Americans don't understand is that Vietnam's not your country.' "

"Yeah."

"It's the Vietnamese people's country."

"Yeah."

"Even the great Niccolò Machiavelli told the Prince something like, 'If you're going to invade, only annex contiguous provinces.' So I would recommend that if we're going to invade anyone, then we should take Canada or Mexico, or forget about it!"

We both laugh.

"You should say that loud and clear," says Dr M. "It is absolutely true. Only annex contiguous provinces—I like that!"

Dr Mahathir continues with his theme that pushing democracy into places where it resists transplantation could hurt more people than the prodigious effort could help. But he also knows that withdrawal from Afghanistan will return that country to its system of feral tribalism.

He adds: "I'm sorry to say, there are countries which will have this kind of problem whether you like it or not. Anymore than you can say, well, China should become democratic. You can't. This is their way. It's their way. Since ancient times, China has been ruled by emperors, and you want to say, 'No, no. You must become democratic!' You know what happens to China if they become democratic? CIVIL WAR."

"A crumbled Yugoslavia?"

"Yes. It will split up. They are different people—the Manchus, the Hokkiens, they are different people. They happen to be geographically in that same area, that is all."

"It'd be a mess?"

"Yeah, it'd be a mess."

"Your view of China is that they have a serious government."

"Yes."

"And that they're making mistakes like any government, but basically they're going in a good direction."

"Yes."

"And that if they stay on that route, in 50 years, they're going to be a really big deal."

"Yes, they will."

"Now, will they gobble up Malaysia, or will you just pay a tribute, or how will that work?"

He waves his hands, as if to push off any doubt: "No, I've always told people that we've been trading with China for 2,000 years. They have never sent an armada to invade us. You know, we traded with the Portuguese in 1509. Two years later, they invaded us and colonized us. So, who are we going to be afraid of?"

"Is that the aggressiveness of Christianity behind that, do you think? Or—"

"Whether it is Christian or not, the European perception of things is different. Even in terms of trading. Immediately after they came here, they wanted a monopoly. They wanted a trade agreement. They wanted to set up forts to defend themselves. They came in armed regiments, whereas the Chinese, the Arabs, the Indians, came here to trade ... since 1,800 years ago, they came to Malaysia to trade. But they never invaded us. They didn't come in armed regiments. They came to trade. So the perception is quite different. The Portuguese, when they came here, they were thinking, 'Well if you have a monopoly of the supplies and this, that and the other, they will become Christian. So, if we have to use force, we'll use force' ... you want some more water?"

Somehow, Dr M has begun to prescribe cold water every time he feels I may be starting to get a little hot under the collar.

Moving on. Dr M's diagnosis of America's problems with the Islamic world is that they derive more from its continued support for Israel's occupation of disputed territories than anything else.

But isn't the Obama administration an improvement?

He says: "Well, he has certain constraints. He can move on other things, he can change things, but on the question of Israel, he is not free to make decisions."

I counter, as if Mr America all of a sudden: "Although, in his 2009 Cairo speech, he spoke a little more frankly, didn't he? I mean, he wasn't doing a Mahathir, but for America he was a third of the way there. It's bizarre."

He answers firmly: "Your country is so powerful, it is very disturbing, because you all need to make decisions which affect the whole world, and yet you know very little about the whole world. And obviously you are going to make wrong decisions. This is the fear of many people, and there were times when you made decisions that were obviously against the general feelings of peoples of the world. You ignored entirely the UN [with Iraq]. It is our hope that the UN would be where we would settle differences, but you said, 'Well I don't care what the UN says, I'm going to go ahead [with the Iraq invasion],' and it's frightening. It's very frightening, because so much depends upon the U.S. president."

"Right, that's right."

"So, this is the thing that worries a lot of people. Others won't say it but I always speak my mind. This is my impression: it's very frightening. You talk about the rule of law, and yet you ignore international law, and you are the one who is going to be looking after the whole world according to the law. If you ignore international law, then how do you preach the rule of law in other countries?"

I ask: "But who can defeat America now? Probably, maybe China in 50 years, but not now. Only America can defeat itself, through internal problems. How do you look at them?"

"It's done so."

"Done what?"

"It has done so; it has defeated itself. You know, this [economic] crisis for example is due to lack of government."

"Lack of government."

"Yeah, and if you look at American cities, you get a feeling that they are decaying. You know, roads are not looked after, bridges are not well maintained. If I want to improve the appearance of Kuala Lumpur, I cannot get any pictures from American cities. I get pictures from Japanese cities to see what they're doing to the street furniture and things like that. Not from America. There are some nice places that you have maintained, but by and large there is a lot of decay in America, as if you don't care anymore. You have reached the top, what is there to do? You see, this is very [*pause*] depressing."

A Mahathir Political Point

Democracy is not easily exportable, and rather than being the answer to a country's problem, may only add to the problem itself.

Casino Royale

Summing up ... a gamble worth taking ... Dr M's missed opportunity, and the West's ... the tragedy

THERE'S no getting around it, for better or for worse—Mahathir has been Malaysia. And his reach and profile on international issues transcends his country. Love him or hate him, he has been a giant of Asia.

Before Mahathir, Malaysia could hardly stake a claim to a serious spot on the serious map of the world. It was mainly viewed, when at all, as a place of cute, small things and warm people suffused in a more or less cozy cultural kampong atmosphere. It was stamped as a sort of nondescript place somewhere between India and the West, and that was about it.

As early as the seventies, in fact, the shadow of Singapore, with its brilliant, articulate, iron-ruling Prime Minister Lee Kuan Yew, spread farther across the globe than much larger and more populous Malaysia. But today, in part because of Dr M's dynamic if deeply controversial 22-year rule, in part because of the West's need to relate better to the Muslim world, and in part because of the rise of a more muscular China in Asia, Malaysia is anything but a geopolitical nonentity.

It also has to be said that modern Malaysia's most successful politician has made many enemies and has many critics. Many Malaysians believe Dr Mahathir presided over a mainly corrupt regime, countenanced poor-quality governance, played foolish footsie with too many crony capitalists, was a phony nationalist, went on far too many ego trips, and was, on the whole, rather a total national embarrassment.

That, in a nutshell, is the unkind take on the good doctor of Malaysia.

But who will history say was the real Dr M? Let us give that tough question a try.

No Prince is ever perfect. Our Leaders, though we hoist them onto pedestals, are not Gods. Far from it, some are monsters.

It is precisely because of the imperfections of any Prince that Niccolò Machiavelli's famous book, *The Prince*, published in 1532, remains such relevant reading even today. He knew leaders were not saints and could not possibly be so: why fool ourselves?

The truth about Princes is that all of them make mistakes but the worst of them are dumb. Even the ones that are very smart might prove to be deeply flawed, lack all moral conviction or abuse their power, whether over their political enemies or over the people under them.

Good old wise Niccolò—the Italian political philosopher still consulted for wisdom and perspective—understood that so well, but was tired of Italian Princes that were ineffective; he thought they'd be the death of any chance for a united Italy. So he would not deal with them as one might wish them to be (saintly) but as they really were (evil and good).

This is key to our assessment of the Machiavellian Muslim Prince at least partly responsible for the contemporary unity of the Malays: the requirement of a standard of near-perfection will lead only to frustration, not enlightenment.

All Princes contain within themselves both good and evil. Our destiny as citizens depends on how that balance (or lack thereof) plays out in our own humble lives. So the most realistic question to be asked by subjects of the Prince (or of the President, or of the Prime Minister) is whether the particular Prince that Fate has bequeathed us is, *on balance*, more good than evil—and how large (and thus helpful to us) is the margin of positivity.

There is no other truly honest question to ask about your Prince. All others are a deception. Ask them to be everywhere and always consistent—same thing. Ask them not to power-lust (or even to spurn the other kind of lust, as we Americans well know), or not to envy, or not to greed—you can try this nice sweet thought on for size, but surely you won't get far with it.

All Princes are imperfect mortals whom we elevate to the altar of the ideal at our self-deceptive peril. But there is a saving grace: at least some of them are effective; at least some do get big things done, markedly improve the lives of their countrymen, boldly point the way to the future, sometimes shove things forward—the latter achieved not infrequently by sheer power of will and political sorcery.

Political will is a phenomenal inexplicable force not much examined under the clinical microscope of the number-crunching political scientist. Until relatively recently, economic or cultural or historical factors were thought to be the only major factors.

But political willpower can make a huge difference.

Consider that, after 9/11, the fear of a global Islamic resurgence swept many parts of the globe. This threw many national leaders off-balance. They did not know how to handle it. In response, one immature, unthinking Prince from the West panicked and even invaded a pair of foreign lands; others withdrew into a shell and acted as if nothing had changed.

But one Prince who had lived with Muslims all his life and who was one himself kept his head about him—and kept it well above the insanities of the moment. In retrospect, this was scant surprise: he had managed a mainly Muslim country for decades. He knew from Islam. He understood their management.

Consider that before this Machiavellian Malay Prince had come to power, ethnic violence roiled in the streets. Many were killed. It was an orgy of destruction that sent a tsunami of shiver across all of Southeast Asia, from Singapore to the south, to Indonesia further south and to the west, to the Philippines to the east. People cannot forget it.

And after this very clever though greatly flawed Prince left power decades later, the otherwise gorgeous and peaceful country of Malaysia re-erupted in a poisonous spate of arson attacks on churches, temples and mosques.

So here is our point: if his 22 years on the job kept things quiet on the Malaysian front while the economy boomed and many more Malaysians lived a better life, how could such a man be all bad?

While nightclubs and hotels and cars and malls were blowing up elsewhere in the region as Islamic violence suddenly brewed into a perfect storm, Malaysia was calm, as if in the eye of the hurricane. Nothing erupted, except economic development. And that made people happy—and made the few outsiders who noticed admiring.

Very little in life happens by accident, unless Mother Nature wills it. Thinking that socio-politial quietude just happens is naïve.

And so it is with this explanation that we have presented to you the riveting, if admittedly complex, saga of Dr Mahathir Mohamad. You have met this strong-willed strongman, this consummate political juggler who became the longest-sitting prime minister in the history of Malaysia. How did he manage to keep his country calm during the storm of the much-advertised clash of civilizations?

You now know some of the answers, and you know them in his own words. He drew on all the brains Allah gave him, all the powers that he could lure into his Office, justifying this power grab as the tacit mandate that he believed the people gave him. In the course of his creation, political institutions were altered and bad things (as well as many good things of course) happened.

But is Malaysia better off today than before the Prince seized the throne? This really isn't much of a question.

That, to me at least, is the standard by which the man must be judged. All the other standards seem either stacked against him, or are academic and thus irrelevant. They also seem parochial.

Note that many critiques focus on the flaws and mistakes of his 22 years solely in terms of his impact on his country. Less attention is paid to his impact outside of Malaysia. And there's a whole big important world out there.

On the plus side, Dr M offered the world a consistent Muslim message: no communal violence internally, no aggressiveness in foreign policy (especially, no forceful efforts to export any political system via violence), and tolerance of all religions (if giving the Jews a hard oral time!). Make economic progress, not war. Let all who think they know who their God is, so worship that god.

Alas, that wasn't the message about Dr Mahathir that reached certain important segments of world public opinion. His caustic, public, pushy, provocative and repetitive criticisms of Israeli government policy in the Middle East and of those Jews and Americans that (in his view) unthinkingly supported Israel led to public-relations disaster for Malaysia in the West. It blurred Malaysia's image, which otherwise would have been formidable, and alienated many who otherwise might have been favorable.

But with his domestic public, his stridency kept the 'ultras' at bay, by fully occupying the political vacuum into which they would have rushed had he opted for a more plain vanilla internationalist line. Any fool could see that his so-called anti-Semitism was little more than a ploy for control of the ultras by surrounding them with the sound of political correctness from the boss man himself.

Had that analysis been more widely understood and accepted, in the Machiavellian sense of acknowledging the ugly compromising realities of oft-nasty human politics, Mahathir's voice might have been heard around the world more prominently—and landed with more instructional value.

That would have enhanced his stature in the Islamic world even more. That this did not happen was, in my view, a major political tragedy.

I don't blame only Mahathir; I also blame the Western news media. It played into the hands of those who wanted Mahathir's views marginalized, precisely because those views were so 'fundamentally' moderate. And who were those people?

They were not the friends of Israel and the West, to say the least.

It was all very, very sad. And very dumb. In a way, Mahathir was the ultimate *anti*-al-Qaeda ... but—keep in mind—one who still had credibility in the Islamic world.

Appendix

He's Much Harder On His Own Muslims Than Those Jews.

Dr M's Prescription For The Islamic World: We Must Get

Our Act Together, We Are Our Own Worst Enemy!

Author's note: The following was one of the more important political speeches of the first decade of the 21st century. It was delivered on October 16, 2003 by Dr Mahathir at the 10th session of the Islamic Summit Conference in Putrajaya, Malaysia.[3] This came near the end of his epic 22-year run as leader of Malaysia's government and was received with an overwhelming ovation. The delivered version ran well beyond 4,000 words. Here is my attempt to condense it, with an occasional comment from me, inserted [like this].

WHETHER [you in this audience] are a Muslim or not, [your] presence at this meeting will help towards greater understanding of Islam and the Muslims, thus helping to disprove the perception of Islam as a religion of backwardness and terror. ... Certainly 1.3 billion Muslims, one-sixth of the world's population, are placing their hopes in us. ...

I will not enumerate the instances of our humiliation and oppression, nor will I once again condemn our detractors and

---

3 Dr Mahathir's full speech can be read on the official website of the Association of Southeast Asian Nations (ASEAN) at http://asean.org/15359.htm

oppressors. It would be an exercise in futility because they are not going to change their attitudes just because we condemn them. If we are to recover our dignity and that of Islam, our religion, it is we who must decide, it is we who must act. ... We are all Muslims. We are all oppressed. We are all being humiliated. ... *[This is NOT rhetoric but how they actually feel and how Dr Mahathir actually feels, even today.]*

Over the last 1,400 years the interpreters of Islam, the learned ones *[quiet sarcasm here]*, the ulamas have interpreted and reinterpreted the single Islamic religion brought by Prophet Muhammad ... so differently that now we have a thousand religions which are often so much at odds with one another that we often fight and kill each other.

From being a single ummah [worldwide community] we have allowed ourselves to be divided into numerous sects ... each more concerned with claiming to be the true Islam than our oneness as the Islamic ummah. *[Dr Mahathir believes Islam as a religion and a culture has been betrayed by religious hyper-intellectuals who have left the community fragmented and thus ripe for conquering.]* We fail to notice that our detractors and enemies do not care whether we are true Muslims or not. To them we are all Muslims, followers of a religion and a Prophet whom they declare promotes terrorism, and we are all their sworn enemies. They will attack and kill us, invade our lands, bring down our Governments whether we are Sunnis or Syiahs, Alawait or Druze or whatever. And we aid and abet them by attacking and weakening each other, and sometimes by doing their bidding, acting as their proxies to attack fellow Muslims. ...

We ignore entirely and we continue to ignore the Islamic injunction to unite and to be brothers to each other.... *[The point being: in the way that—he believes—Jews are a community more united than Muslims are.]* But this is not all that we ignore about the teachings of Islam. We are enjoined to Read, *Iqraq* i.e. to acquire knowledge. The early Muslims took this to mean translating and studying the works of the Greeks and other scholars before Islam. And these Muslim scholars added to the body of knowledge through their own studies.

The early Muslims produced great mathematicians and scientists, scholars, physicians and astronomers etc. and they excelled in all the fields of knowledge of their times, besides studying and practicing their own religion of Islam. As a result the Muslims were able to develop and extract wealth from their lands and through their world trade, able to strengthen their defenses, protect their people and give them the Islamic way of life.... *[This is what is today so missed and wanted.]* At the time the Europeans of the Middle Ages were still superstitious and backward, the enlightened Muslims had already built a great Muslim civilization, respected and powerful, more than able to compete with the rest of the world and able to protect the ummah from foreign aggression. The Europeans had to kneel at the feet of Muslim scholars in order to access their own scholastic heritage. ... *[Ah, the good old-old-old days!]*

But halfway through the building of the great Islamic civilization came new interpreters of Islam who taught that acquisition of knowledge by Muslims meant only the study of Islamic theology. The study of science, medicine etc. was discouraged. Intellectually the Muslims began to regress. With intellectual regression the great Muslim civilization began to falter and wither. ...

With all these developments over the centuries, the ummah and the Muslim civilization became so weak that at one time there was not a single Muslim country which was not colonized or hegemonized by the Europeans. But regaining independence did not help to strengthen the Muslims. Their states were weak and badly administered, constantly in a state of turmoil. The Europeans could do what they liked with Muslim territories. It is not surprising that they should excise Muslim land to create the state of Israel to solve their Jewish problem. Divided, the Muslims could do nothing effective to stop the Balfour and Zionist transgression. *[This is the core of his animosity toward Israel and its great ally the U.S.—Muslim impotence.]*

Some would have us believe that, despite all these, our life is better than that of our detractors. Some believe that poverty is Islamic, sufferings and being oppressed are Islamic. This world is not for us. Ours are the joys of heaven in the afterlife. All that we have to do is to perform certain rituals, wear certain garments and put up a certain appearance. Our weakness, our backwardness and our inability to help our brothers and sisters who are being oppressed are part of the Will of Allah, the sufferings that we must endure before enjoying heaven in the hereafter. We must accept this fate that befalls us. We need not do anything. We can do nothing against the Will of Allah. *[At this point reports had it that he had the audience of Muslim leaders on their feet stomping and cheering—the master politician at the top of his game.]*

But is it true that it is the Will of Allah and that we can and should do nothing? Allah has said in *Surah Ar-Ra'd* verse 11 that He will not change the fate of a community until the community has tried to change its fate itself.

The early Muslims were as oppressed as we are presently. But after their sincere and determined efforts to help themselves in accordance with the teachings of Islam, Allah had helped them to defeat their enemies and to create a great and powerful Muslim civilization. But what effort have we made especially with the resources that He has endowed us with?

We are now 1.3 billion strong. We have the biggest oil reserve in the world. We have great wealth. ... We are familiar with the workings of the world's economy and finances. We control 57 out of the 180 countries in the world. Our votes can make or break international organizations. Yet we seem ... helpless.... Why? Is it because of Allah's Will or is it because we have interpreted our religion wrongly, or failed to abide by the correct teachings of our religion, or done the wrong things? *[Again, he does not blame 'Jews' but hints at betrayal by far-out Muslim theologians for creating Islamic chaos.]*

We are enjoined by our religion to prepare for the defense of the ummah. Unfortunately we stress not defense but the weapons of the time of the Prophet. Those weapons and horses cannot help to defend us anymore. We need guns and rockets, bombs and warplanes, tanks and warships for our defense. But because we discouraged the learning of science and mathematics etc. ..., today we have no capacity to produce our own weapons for our defense. We have to buy our weapons from our detractors and enemies. *[See how the Islamic world suffers when it listens to 'strict constructionist' theologians!]* This is what comes from the superficial interpretation of the Quran, stressing not the substance of the Prophet's sunnah [the ways, teachings and activities of the Prophet] and the Quran's injunctions but rather the form…. And it is the same with the other teachings of Islam. We are more concerned with the forms rather than the substance of the words of Allah and adhering only to the literal interpretation of the traditions of the Prophet.

… Our detractors and enemies will take advantage of the resulting backwardness and weakness in order to dominate us. Islam is not just for the 7th century AD. Islam is for all times. And times have changed. … Islam is not wrong but the interpretations by our scholars, who are not prophets, even though they may be very learned, can be wrong. We have a need to go back to the fundamental teachings of Islam to find out whether we are indeed believing in and practicing the Islam that the Prophet preached. It cannot be that we are all practicing the correct and true Islam when our beliefs are so different from one another. … *[In other words: who's responsible for this mess?]*

None of our countries are truly independent. We are under pressure to conform to our oppressors' wishes about how we should behave, how we should govern our lands, how we should think even. Today if they want to raid our country, kill our people, destroy our villages and towns, there is nothing substantial that we can do. Is it Islam which has caused all these? Or is it that we have failed to do our duty according to our religion?

Our only reaction is to become more and more angry. Angry people cannot think properly. And so we find some of our people reacting irrationally. They launch their own attacks, killing just about anybody including fellow Muslims to vent their anger and frustration. *[Dr Mahathir is obviously no fan of Muslim terrorism at all—but this has been largely lost on much of the West, alas.]* Their Governments can do nothing to stop them. The enemy retaliates and puts more pressure on the Governments. And the Governments have no choice but to give in, to accept the directions of the enemy, literally to give up their independence of action.

With this their people and the ummah become angrier and turn against their own Governments. Every attempt at a peaceful solution is sabotaged by more indiscriminate attacks calculated to anger the enemy and prevent any peaceful settlement. But the attacks solve nothing. The Muslims simply get more oppressed. *[From his perspective, 9/11 was so colossally stupid, you almost have to think it had to have been masterminded by enemies of Islam. Can you follow his logic—or at least the emotion of it?]*

There is a feeling of hopelessness among the Muslim countries and their people. ... But is it true that we should do and can do nothing for ourselves? Is it true that 1.3 billion people can exert no power to save themselves from the humiliation and oppression inflicted upon them by a much smaller enemy? Can they only lash back blindly in anger? Is there no other way than to ask our young people to blow themselves up and kill people and invite the massacre of more of our own people? *[He is a philosophical pacifist and a pragmatic advocate of nonviolence in the great Gandhi tradition.]*

It cannot be that there is no other way. 1.3 billion Muslims cannot be defeated by a few million Jews. *[By 'defeat', he means 'bested' or 'bettered'. But the emotional impact of being 'defeated' again and again sours the Muslim world and turns it into a 'defeatist' community, he thinks.]* There must be a way. ... Surely the 23 years' struggle of the Prophet can provide us with some guidance as to what we can and should do.

We know he and his early followers were oppressed.... Did he launch retaliatory strikes? No. He was prepared to make strategic retreats. ...he was prepared to accept an unfair treaty, against the wishes of his companions and followers. *[That is, for example, Arafat was unwise not to have taken that deal brokered by Bill Clinton.]* During the peace that followed he consolidated his strength and eventually he was able to enter Mecca and claim it for Islam. Even then he did not seek revenge. And the peoples of Mecca accepted Islam and many became his most powerful supporters, defending the Muslims against all their enemies. ...

If we use the faculty to think that Allah has given us, then we should know that we are acting irrationally. We fight without any objective, without any goal other than to hurt the enemy because they hurt us. Naïvely we expect them to surrender. We sacrifice lives unnecessarily, achieving nothing other than to attract more massive retaliation and humiliation. *[Isn't this interesting? Too bad Hamas and others don't find his logic compelling.]*

... For well over half a century we have fought over Palestine.

What have we achieved? Nothing. We are worse off than before. If we had paused to think then we could have devised a plan, a strategy that can win us final victory. Pausing and thinking calmly is not a waste of time. We have a need to make a strategic retreat and to calmly assess our situation. *[A strategy of an 'eye-for-an-eye' is not a strategy; it's a brainless formula for a kind of insane political repetitive-stress syndrome.]*

We are actually very strong. 1.3 billion people cannot be simply wiped out. The Europeans killed six million Jews out of 12 million. But today the Jews rule this world by proxy. They get others to fight and die for them. *[Such as the United States.]*

We may not be able to do that. We may not be able to unite all the 1.3 billion Muslims. We may not be able to get all the Muslim Governments to act in concert. But even if we can get a third of the ummah and a third of the Muslim states to act together, we can already do something. ... *[He is not saying he wants Jews decimated, he is pointing out that, for all their losses, they have renewed themselves powerfully; so why can't Muslims stand up together for their own interests?]*

We also know that not all non-Muslims are against us. Some are well disposed towards us. Some even see our enemies as their enemies. Even among the Jews there are many who do not approve of what the Israelis are doing. *[Which is precisely why any concept—in his mind or elsewhere—of a 'coherent' Jewish or Israeli 'community' is a fiction.]*

We must not antagonize everyone. We must win their hearts and minds. We must win them to our side not by begging for help from them but by the honorable way that we struggle to help ourselves. We must not strengthen the enemy by pushing everyone into their camps through irresponsible and un-Islamic acts. ... Remember the considerateness of the Prophet to the enemies of Islam. We must do the same. It is winning the struggle that is important, not angry retaliation, not revenge. *[Let's start playing it smart.]*

We must build up our strength in every field, not just in armed might. Our countries must be stable and well administered, must be economically and financially strong, industrially competent and technologically advanced. This will take time, but it can be done and it will be time well spent. ...

To do the things that are suggested will not even require all of us to give up our differences with each other. We need only to call a truce so we can act together in tackling only certain problems of common interests, the Palestine problem for example.

In any struggle, in any war, nothing is more important than concerted and coordinated action. A degree of discipline is all that is needed. ... The Quran tells us that when the enemy sues for peace we must react positively. True the treaty offered is not favorable to us. But we can negotiate. The Prophet did, at Hudaibiyah. And in the end he triumphed. *[Stop rejecting these offers; half a loaf is much better than none!]*

I am aware that all these ideas will not be popular. Those who are angry would want to reject it out of hand. They would even want to silence anyone who makes or supports this line of action. They would want to send more young men and women to make the supreme sacrifice. But where will all these lead to? Certainly not victory. Over the past 50 years of fighting in Palestine we have not achieved any result. We have in fact worsened our situation.

The enemy will probably welcome these proposals and we will conclude that the promoters are working for the enemy. But think. We are up against a people who think. They survived 2,000 years of pogroms not by hitting back, but by thinking. They invented and successfully promoted Socialism, Communism, human rights and democracy so that persecuting them would appear to be wrong, so they may enjoy equal rights with others. With these they have now gained control of the most powerful countries and they, this tiny community, have become a world power. We cannot fight them through brawn alone. We must use our brains also.

Of late because of their power and their apparent success they have become arrogant. And arrogant people, like angry people, will make mistakes, will forget to think. *[Which he doesn't want to happen to his people.]*

They are already beginning to make mistakes. And they will make more mistakes. There may be windows of opportunity for us now and in the future. We must seize these opportunities. But to do so we must get our acts right … The power we (leaders) wield is for our people, for the ummah, for Islam. We must have the will to make use of this power judiciously, prudently, concertedly. Insyaallah we will triumph in the end. *[The bottom line: if we don't act on our behalf, who will?]*

Author's Methodology Note

All of the quotations attributed to Dr Mahathir and myself are almost exactly as they took place over four separate interviews in 2009 and 2010, though not in the exact order of their occurrence, of course. Arranged for thematic reasons, they were recorded on flipshare video cameras and were professionally transcribed. However, a certain number (but not all) of the "hmms" and "you knows" and "wells" and "so ons" were cleaned out. The normal detritus of actual human conversation is heard on one wavelength but can appear to be on an entirely different wavelength when written down in words. To suggest in any way, by stubbornly insisting on overly literal transcriptions of our conversations, that Dr Mahathir was anything but extremely articulate would be a grave disservice to the reader and a profound journalistic inaccuracy. And so these "hmms" were mostly removed in order to present a more truthful picture of—and impression of—our exchanges.

Works Consulted and Recommended

Abdullah, Ahmad. *Dr Mahathir's Selected Letters to World Leaders.* Marshall Cavendish: Singapore, 2008 [Some vintage Mahathir here, alternatively humble, wry and pushy]

Arrighi, Giovanni. *Adam Smith in Beijing.* Verso: London, 2007 [The most amazing political-economic transformation in recent history]

Backman, Michael. *Asia Future Shock: Business Crises and Opportunity in the Coming Years.* Palgrave Macmillan: New York, 2008 [Problems for Malaysia in the future, he says]

Crooke, Alastair. *Resistance: The Essence of the Islamist Revolution.* Pluto Press: London, New York, 2009 [Partisan, pro-Islamic, but brilliant and, precisely because of its tilt, refreshing for Western eyes]

Gowan, Peter. *The Global Gamble.* Verso: London, 1999 [Prescient analysis of what went wrong in the 90s, prefiguring the next decade]

Hasan, Zoya (editor). *Democracy in Muslim Societies.* Sage Publications: New Delhi, 2007 [A useful and very solid primer]

Johnson, Paul. *Modern Times: The World From the Twenties to the Nineties.* Revised Edition. HarperPerennial: New York, 1992 [A masterpiece, basically a subtle argument for extreme caution in political change]

Khoo, Boo Teik. *Beyond Mahathir.* Zed Books: London, New York, 2003 [One of the best studies about Mahathir in English]

Khoo, Boo Teik. *Paradoxes of Mahathirism: An Intellectual Biography of Mahathir Mohamad.* Oxford University Press, Oxford, New York, 1995 [Same as immediately above]

Mahathir Mohamad, Shintaro Ishihara. *The Voice of Asia.* Kodanasha International: Tokyo, 1995 [Silly, immature, odd, but very important]

Mahathir Mohamad. *The Malay Dilemma.* Marshall Cavendish: Singapore, 2008 [His seminal work, written at the outset of his extraordinary political career and first published in 1970]

Wain, Barry. *Malaysian Maverick: Mahathir Mohamad in Turbulent Times.* Pargrave Macmillan: New York 2009 [Definitive, encompassing; a must-read to understand the Mahathir years]

About the Author

TOM Plate is an American journalist whose international career has seen him working at media institutions from London to Los Angeles. Born in New York, he completed his studies at Amherst College (cum laude, Phi Beta Kappa) and Princeton University's Woodrow Wilson School of Public and International Affairs, where he earned his master's degree in public and international affairs. His syndicated columns focusing on Asia and America have run often in major newspapers in Dubai, Singapore, Hong Kong, Seoul, Tokyo, Providence (Rhode Island) and other U.S. outlets.

He has received awards from the American Society of Newspaper Editors, the California Newspaper Publishers Association and the Greater Los Angeles Press Club. In 1993, when he was Editor of the Editorial Pages, the *Los Angeles Times* garnered the Pulitzer Prize for its coverage of the Los Angeles riots.

From 1994 to 2008, he taught in the communication and policy studies departments at the University of California, Los Angeles. He has been a Media Fellow at Stanford University and a fellow in Tokyo at the Japanese Foreign Press Center's annual Asia-Pacific Media Conference. He is currently Distinguished Scholar of Asian and Pacific Studies at Loyola Marymount University, Los Angeles.

He was the founder of the non-profit Asia Pacific Media Network (APMN), whose webpages migrated to the University of Southern California (USC) as 'AsiaMedia' and 'Asia Pacific Arts'. He also founded and is currently director of the Pacific Perspectives Media Center in Beverly Hills, California, a non-profit organization under APMN that syndicates high-end op-eds and manages a website 'Pacific Perspectives Front Page' (pacificpersepectives. blogspot.com).

On the West Coast, he is a board member of the Pacific Century Institute and a Senior Fellow at the USC Center for the Digital Future, as well as a long-standing member of the World Affairs Council of Los Angeles and the Pacific Council on International Policy; on the East Coast he is a long-standing member of the Princeton Club of New York, the Century Association (recently resigned) and the Phi Beta Kappa Society.

Tom is also the author of seven books, including *Confessions of an American Media Man* (Marshall Cavendish 2007), now into its second edition, and *Conversations with Lee Kuan Yew* (2010). For years he was a participant at the retreats of the World Economic Forum in Davos, Switzerland.

He resides in Beverly Hills with his wife Andrea, a licensed clinical social worker, and their three cats.